M000232006

Advance Praise for *Electronic and Algorithmic Trading Technology*

"Kendall Kim's *Electronic and Algorithmic Trading Technology* is well written, thoroughly researched, and logically organized. I look forward to using the book as a resource for class."
  —**Dr. Scott Gibson**, *Professor of Finance at the William & Mary Mason School of Business*

"In *Electronic and Algorithmic Trading Technology*, Kendall Kim provides valuable insight into the highly specialized world of computer trading. This includes key terminology and definitions, regulatory background, and industry drivers. In addition, the book provides an overview of the technologies and methodologies that comprise this complex industry. *Electronic and Algorithmic Trading Technology* is roadmap to the world of computer trading and is essential reading for both buy- and sell-side market participants."
  —**Sean Gilman**, *CTO, Currenex*

"Kendall Kim has managed to give a comprehensive overview of the mechanisms, the competitive landscape, and even some forecasts on the complex and quickly evolving topic of electronic and algorithmic trading technology. Deep domain knowledge is critical to success on Wall Street; understanding complex market forces at work only enhances the value one can bring to their trade. Anyone who wants to learn more about this rapidly evolving phenomenon can benefit by reading Kendall's book."
  —**Jeff Hudson**, *CEO, Vhayu Technologies Corporation*

"Comprehensive and up-to-date. Useful for both practioners and academics."
  —**George S. Oldfield**, *Principal, The Brattle Group Washington, D.C.*

"*Electronic and Algorithmic Trading Technology*" is an excellent resource for both academics and financial professionals outside the domain of electronic trading who are seeking a comprehensive review of an increasingly complex and ever-changing trading landscape. Kendall Kim has managed to provide an insightful, engaging, and eminently accessible summary of the core elements of algorithmic and electronic trading, the challenges faced by all trading businesses today, and what lies in store for the future of trading across a multitude of asset classes."
  —**Manny Santayana**, *Managing Director Advanced Execution Services – Equities, Credit Suisse*

"Kendall Kim's work is a thorough snapshot of the world of automated trading, with an intricate history explaining why and how we got where we are today. Packed with examples and anecdotes, it makes an impressive reference guide to the multitudes of algorithms, systems and regulations in existence across the globe."
  —**Matthew J Smalley**, *Director – ETD Execution Technology, UBS Investment Bank*

Complete Technology Guides for Financial Services Series

Series Editors

Ayesha Kaljuvee and Jürgen Kaljuvee

Series Description

Industry pressures to shorten trading cycles and provide information-on-demand are forcing firms to re-evaluate and re-engineer all operations. Shortened trading cycles will put additional emphasis on improving risk management through front-, middle-, and back-office operations. Both business and IT managers need to effectively translate these requirements into systems using the latest technologies and the best frameworks.

The books in the **Complete Technology Guides for Financial Services Series** outline the way to create and judge technology solutions that meet business requirements through a robust decision-making process. Whether your focus is technical or operational, internal or external, front, middle, or back office, or buy vs. build, these books provide the framework for designing a cutting-edge technology solution to fit your needs.

We welcome proposals for books for the series. Readers interested in learning more about the series and Elsevier books in finance, including how to submit proposals for books in the series, can go to: http://www.books.elsevier.com/finance

Electronic and Algorithmic Trading Technology

The Complete Guide

Kendall Kim

ELSEVIER

AMSTERDAM • BOSTON • HEIDELBERG • LONDON
NEW YORK • OXFORD • PARIS • SAN DIEGO
SAN FRANCISCO • SINGAPORE • SYDNEY • TOKYO

Academic Press is an imprint of Elsevier

Academic Press in an imprint of Elsevier
30 Corporate Drive, Suite 400, Burlington, MA 01803, USA
525 B Street, Suite 1900, San Diego, California 92101-4495, USA
84 Theobald's Road, London WC1X 8RR, UK

This book is printed on acid-free paper. ∞

Library of Congress Cataloging-in Publication Data
Kim, Kendall.
    Electronic and algorithmic trading technology : the complete guide / Kendall Kim. — 1st ed.
        p. cm.
    Includes bibliographical references and index.
    ISBN: 978-0-12-372491-5 (pbk. : alk. paper)   1.   Stocks—Prices—Mathematical models.
2.   Programs trading (Securities) 3.   Stock exchanges. I.   Title.
    HG4636.K55 2007
    332.64—dc22

                                                                        2007013849

British Library Cataloguing in Publication Data
A catalogue record for this book is available from the British Library

ISBN: 978-0-12-372491-5

For information on all Academic Press Publications
visit our Web site at www.books.elsevier.com

Printed in the United States of America
08   09   10   11   9   8   7   6   5   4   3   2

Special thanks to Sang Lee of the Aite Group as well as Larry Tabb and Marty Rabkin of the TABB Group whose valuable contributions and generosity have made this book possible.

Contents

About the Author   xiii

Series Preface
                                                                        xv
Introduction   xix

CHAPTER 1

Overview of Electronic and Algorithmic Trading   1

  1.1 Overview   1

  1.2 The Emergence of Electronic Trading Networks   2

  1.3 The Participants   4

  1.4 The Impact of Decimalization   6

  1.5 The Different Faces of Electronic Trading   8

  1.6 Program Trading and the Stock Market Crash of 1987   10

  1.7 Conclusion   13

CHAPTER 2

Automating Trade and Order Flow   15

  2.1 Introduction   15

2.2   Internal Controls   16

2.3   Trade Cycle   17

2.4   Straight-Through Processing and Trade Automation   19

2.5   Data Management   20

2.6   Order Management Systems   22

2.7   Order Routing   25

2.8   Liquidity Shift   26

2.9   Conclusion   28

CHAPTER 3

The Growth of Program and Algorithmic Trading   **29**

3.1   Introduction   29

3.2   A Sample Program Trade   31

3.3   The Downside of Program Trading   33

3.4   Market Growth and IT Spending   36

3.5   Conclusion   38

CHAPTER 4

Alternative Execution Venues   **39**

4.1   Introduction   39

4.2   Structure of Exchanges   40

4.3   Rule 390   43

4.4   Exchanges Scramble to Consolidate   44

4.5   Arguments Against Exchanges   44

4.6   The Exchanges in the News   46

4.7   Conclusion   49

CHAPTER 5

Algorithmic Strategies   **51**

5.1   Introduction   51

5.2 Algorithmic Penetration 52

5.3 Implementation Shortfall Measurement 54

5.4 Volume-Weighted Average Price 56

5.5 VWAP Definitions 58

5.6 Time-Weighted Average Price 60

5.7 Conclusion 62

CHAPTER 6

Algorithmic Feasibility and Limitations 63

6.1 Introduction 63

6.2 Trade Structure 64

6.3 Algorithmic Feasibility 64

6.4 Algorithmic Trading Checklist 66

6.5 High Opportunity Cost 67

6.6 Newsflow Algorithms 68

6.7 Black Box Trading for Fixed-Income Instruments 69

6.8 Conclusion 70

CHAPTER 7

Electronic Trading Networks 71

7.1 Introduction 71

7.2 Direct Market Access 71

7.3 Electronic Communication Networks 75

7.4 Shifting Trends 79

7.5 Conclusion 80

CHAPTER 8

Effective Data Management 83

8.1 Introduction 83

8.2 Real-Time Data   84

8.3 Strategy Enablers   85

8.4 Order Routing   87

8.5 Impact on Operations and Technology   88

8.6 Conclusion   89

CHAPTER 9

Minimizing Execution Costs   **91**

9.1 Introduction   91

9.2 Components of Trading Costs   92

9.3 Price Impacts with Liquidity   93

9.4 Cost of Waiting   97

9.5 Explicit Costs—Commissions, Fees, and Taxes   98

9.6 Conclusion   100

CHAPTER 10

Transaction Cost Research   **103**

10.1 Introduction   103

10.2 Post-Trade TCR   105

10.3 Pre-Trade TCR   106

10.4 The Future of Transaction Cost Research   108

10.5 Conclusion   109

CHAPTER 11

Electronic and Algorithmic Trading for Different Asset Classes **111**

11.1 Introduction   111

11.2 Development of Electronic Trading   113

11.3 Electronic Trading Platforms   116

11.4 Types of Systems   119

11.5   TRACE—Reform in Transparency   120

11.6   Foreign Exchange Markets   122

11.7   The FX Market Ecosystem   123

11.8   Conclusion   124

CHAPTER 12

Regulation NMS and Other Regulatory Reporting   **125**

12.1   Introduction   125

12.2   Regulatory Challenges   126

12.3   The National Market System   127

12.4   The Impact of Regulatory NMS   131

12.5   Markets in Financial Instruments Directive in Europe   133

12.6   Regulatory and Exchange Reporting   135

12.7   Example of an Exchange Data Processing System   138

12.8   Conclusion   139

CHAPTER 13

Build vs. Buy   **141**

13.1   Introduction   141

13.2   Vendor as a Service Provider   143

13.3   Striving to Stand Out   147

13.4   The Surge of Electronic Trading Through
       Regulatory Changes   149

13.5   Hedge Fund Systems—Outsource or In-House?   149

13.6   Conclusion   152

CHAPTER 14

Trading Technology and Prime Brokerage   **153**

14.1   Introduction   153

14.2   Prime Broker Services   154

14.3   The Structure of Hedge Funds   157
14.4   The Impact of Increased Trade Automation   158
14.5   Different Markets and Asset Classes   159
14.6   The Prime Brokerage Market   160
14.7   Conclusion   161

CHAPTER 15
Profiling the Leading Vendors   **163**
15.1   Introduction   163
15.2   Profiling Leading Vendors   166
15.3   Order Management Systems   175

Appendix: The Implementation of Trading Systems   **181**
Glossary of Terms   **187**
Index   **199**

About the Author

Kendall Kim is a Business Analyst based out of New York City and lives in Connecticut. He specializes in delivering technology solutions to Wall Street securities firms. In this role he has been responsible for the specification and implementation of large trading, risk management, and real-time market data systems. Kendall holds a bachelor's degree in Economics from Boston University, Boston, MA and a master's degree in Business Administration from The College of William and Mary, Williamsburg, VA.

Series Preface

Kendall Kim's book *Electronic and Algorithmic Trading Technology* is an important addition to the **Complete Technology Guides for Financial Services Series**, the first series of its kind to focus specifically on financial technology trends, challenges, and their solutions. The book could not have come to the market at a more opportune moment. The financial trading industry, with broker-dealers, buy-side funds, exchanges, and venues of trade execution as its primary players, is experiencing a historical transformation. This enormous change is being driven by deep underlying factors shaping global markets today, including (1) the consolidation of execution venues and the birth of global exchanges, (2) competitive pressures on broker-dealers to offer electronic services and best order execution to their clients, and (3) increased regulatory requirements from financial authorities to improve transparency for all market participants.

Before reviewing some of the highlights in the chapters of this new and exciting book, a note of clarification on basic terminology is in order. When talking about the evolution of trading technology, it is important to distinguish among electronic trading, program trading, and algorithmic trading. Electronic trading refers to connecting the trade counterparties to one another through an electronic execution protocol and eliminating what was known as voice brokerage. This wave of innovation began in the 1980s and is still taking place. Secondly, program trading refers to the requirement of executing large baskets of shares. Finally, algorithmic trading, in its simplest (but not all-inclusive) definition, refers to algorithms for breaking down blocks of trade orders to obtain best price and execution while minimizing market impact. In a way, these are also the basic three steps of the evolution of trading with most market participants continuing to innovate and grow in all three dimensions. Note that this maturation is taking place both in terms of technology as well as financial modeling and analytics, since they go hand in hand. Kendall Kim's book discusses all three areas of trade automation and innovation in detail, with particular focus on electronic and algorithmic trading, providing research figures and statistics throughout to enrich the reader's experience.

The first three chapters of the book introduce the reader to key concepts, the trade life cycle, and factors driving the growth of electronic trading in recent years. The book begins with *Chapter 1: Overview of Electronic and Algorithmic Trading*, which defines important ideas and gives a historical perspective on the emergence of program and algorithmic trading. We learn how decimalization, which changed the way the New York Stock Exchange quoted security prices, impacted the market, and how Electronic Communication Networks (ECNs) and multilateral trading facilities (MTFs) emerged to compete with monopolistic central exchanges. The chapter covers different aspects of electronic trading, such as duration averaging, dynamic hedging, and index arbitrage, and touches on the connectivity protocol known as FIX (Financial Information Exchange), which is the technological basis for increased connectivity. *Chapter 2: Automating Trade and Order Flow* covers the trade life cycle from beginning to end. It highlights the major steps in the trade life cycle, such as trade confirmation, settlement, and reconciliation. It argues that changing back-office processes are, in fact, key enablers of financial innovation. It gives perspective on the automation of trading from both a technology and a management point of view, describing important concepts such as direct market access (DMA), smart order routing, and straight-through processing (STP). *Chapter 3: The Growth of Program and Algorithmic Trading* reviews statistics like average daily volume (ADV) whose exploding number is attributable to the rising prevalence of program and algorithmic trading. The chapter also studies the correlation between the rise in program trading and the increase in IT spending in the financial services industry.

Chapter 4: Alternative Execution Venues explains the drivers behind the need for these new venues, such as speed of execution, regulatory pressures, cost savings, direct market access (DMA), and the desire for anonymity. The chapter compares the electronic trading networks to exchanges, and discusses economic disadvantages of the latter, including factors like monopoly and externalities, which created the need for alternative securities markets. Finally, it reviews various exchanges globally that are likely to be most affected by the growth of execution venues.

Chapter 5: Algorithmic Strategies describes the major algorithms in detail, with an eye on the goal of each strategy. The reader learns basic concepts like implementation shortfall and execution benchmarks such as VWAP (Volume-Weighted Average Pricing) and TWAP (Time-Weighted Average Pricing). The chapter shows how market practitioners use these algorithms, and shows which market participants offer the best strategy executions. *Chapter 6: Algorithmic Feasibility and Limitations* takes the topic of algorithms further, introducing the central notion of transaction cost analysis (TCA). The reader is introduced to a set of analytical tools, with a framework for deciding which types of algorithms are suited to which objective of a trader or investor. *Chapter 7: Electronic Trading Networks* tackles the new set of liquidity providers know as Electronic Communication Networks (ECN) and multilateral trading facilities (MTF). It goes into more detail regarding shifting trends and direct market access (DMA) technology. *Chapter 8: Effective Data Management* emphasizes the importance of having a strategy in place for managing this data, especially given the value of detailed and clean data for any kind of accurate analysis. *Chapter 9: Minimizing Execution Costs* and *Chapter 10: Transaction Cost Research* delve into the details of minimizing costs associated with any kind of trader execution, covering both the explicit and implicit costs. They also provide a wide range of market statistics on how the cost varies depending on the market, order type, and size of the order.

It comes as little surprise that equity markets were the first ones to adopt this type of trading, but what about other major asset classes such as fixed income, foreign exchange, and commodities? *Chapter 11: Electronic and Algorithmic Trading for Different Asset Classes* reviews how electronic trading has taken ground depending on the asset class in question, providing some interesting and revealing answers to which classes are most likely to be affected next and how your area in the industry might be changed by it.

Of course, every part of the industry, including the new asset classes entering into the electronic trading world, is impacted by regulatory reporting requirements set in place by financial authorities. *Chapter 12: Regulation NMS and Other Regulatory Reporting* examines the philosophy behind compliance and regulatory laws, describing various types of reporting such as electronic blue sheets, Regulation NMS, and DPTR in the United States and MiFID in Europe. It reviews who is affected by these requirements and the mechanisms by which an organization can prepare itself to meet them.

The last three chapters of the book introduce the technology aspects of electronic and algorithmic trading in detail, starting with the technologies undertaken by vendors and prime brokers. *Chapter 13: Build vs. Buy* investigates what goes into the all-important decision-making process of determining whether to build or buy electronic-trading-related technologies, providing readers with the basic principles and criteria under which such decisions should be made. Prime brokers are sell-side players that offer leverage, trade processing, and clearance services for buy-side firms, such as hedge funds, and are strong participants in the electronic and algorithmic trading arena. It is then not surprising that prime brokers are often at the forefront of providing electronic and algorithmic solutions, both analytically and technologically, particularly on the back end. *Chapter 14: Trading Technology and Prime Brokerage* gives the reader an insider view of how these players build their electronic trading technology. Given the speed of electronic execution and the number of transactions occurring per day, technologists have to consider how to deal with the enormous amounts of financial data being generated by electronic trading. Finally, the book ends with *Chapter 15: Profiling the Leading Vendors* and gives the reader the tools to "go algorithmic," as it is often said in the industry, right after reading the book, that is, today or in the worst case, tomorrow.

In summary, Kendall Kim's *Electronic and Algorithmic Trading Technology* is a unique book both in terms of the level of detail as well as the breadth of its scope. If you are a senior manager at a sell-side or a buy-side firm, an execution venue; or a broker, regulator, or fund manager in charge of implementing technology systems for your business; or just curious about where the future of finance is heading, this book provides key insights and guidance on the fundamentals of electronic trading and the technological solutions for implementing them.

Series Editors

Ayesha Kaljuvee
New York, USA

Jürgen Kaljuvee
London, UK

Introduction

The objective of this book is to educate financial service professionals responsible for developing, managing, and implementing cutting-edge trade technology. It also provides a guide to institutional investors, broker-dealers, and software vendors with a better understanding of innovative enhancements that can cut transaction costs, minimize human error, boost trading efficiency, and supplement productivity. Economic and regulatory pressures also have an effect in improving technology. Regulation NMS, and the fundamental principle of obtaining the best price for investors when such price is immediately accessible, rather than executing a listed stock solely through an exchange is one regulatory enhancement. Electronic and algorithmic trading is increasingly becoming a mainstream response to institutional investors' needs to move large blocks of shares with fewer transaction costs, negligible market impact, and information leakage. Constant innovations designed to cut costs and create new efficiencies in the securities industry have forced investment banking firms as well as institutional investment advisors to rethink their trading operations. Algorithms are clearly cost-effective methods for executing low-maintenance equity trades. They have led to head-count shifts and reductions in sales and trading desks. These automated trades can meet the demand of customers who want lower transaction costs. The growth of new technologies in electronic and algorithmic trading has created a new industry for financial professionals. Appropriate protocols and efficient process infrastructure are required to help grow this industry. Investment banks, agency brokers, and investment managers require efficient front-to-back securities processing cycles to make this happen. The whole trade process, which includes execution, confirmation, and reconciliation, has to be in place in order for trades to occur. This book will cover in more detail how this process flow is structured.

Chapter 1

Overview of Electronic and Algorithmic Trading

1.1 Overview

Electronic and algorithmic trading has become a significantly larger focus for financial institutions, securities regulators, and different exchanges. Market developments along with tougher regulations have made equity trading more complicated and less profitable. Automation and new technologies have changed the trading game dramatically in the past five years or so. The speed of financial information is outpacing anyone's forecast. Higher networking speeds through financial engineering are altering the way traders and market participants address the demand for lower commissions and enabling the creation of automated model-based trading. The increase in competition for lower transaction costs has been forcing firms to invest significantly in their trading and processing infrastructure. The proliferation of electronic and algorithmic trading has been staggering on Wall Street. A broker can no longer fulfill order flow without using some method of electronic execution. The traditional clerks running across the trading floor with order slips and men in pits negotiating bid prices may soon be replaced by the sound of traders typing in their parameters onto their broker screens to facilitate order flow using programs and algorithms. In the past, there were limited opportunities to apply technology to the trading process or interact directly with exchanges and market participants. This has all changed with the introduction of programs, direct market access, and algorithmic trading. Although automated trade flow can carry connotations of computerized trading taking over without human supervision, the actual decisions to buy and sell are made by people, not computers. Humans make the final trading decisions and the parameters behind implementing them, but computers may calculate algorithms that route the order flow efficiently and in many cases, computers help the breakdown of trades to each individual stock within the program.

1.2 The Emergence of Electronic Trading Networks

Algorithmic trading has become another method for large brokerage firms to grasp an advantage over their competitors for lower-cost executions; however, smaller players such as agency brokers also see algorithms as a way to level the playing field and infringe on the bigger bulge-bracket firms. Algorithmic trading originated on proprietary trading desks of investment banking firms. It began to expand executing client orders because of new markets and the need to remain in line with new players in the brokerage industry. This has created a more competitive environment for traditional dealers with services such as direct market access through the Internet. According to Manny Santayana, managing director at Credit Suisse's Advanced Execution Services Group (AES), "Algorithmic trading has created a level playing field which ultimately benefits shareholders with smarter, more efficient, and cheaper execution." NASDAQ and other electronic exchanges have threatened the traditional model of the New York Stock Exchange with their phone-based order flow, and its utilization of floor brokers.

In 2001, the Securities and Exchange Commission imposed decimalization. This mandate forced market makers and buy-side institutions to switch from valuing stocks in traditional sixteenths ($.0625) to valuing them in penny spreads ($.01), which increased price points from 6 for every dollar to 100. Trading margins have been significantly reduced by 84% as a result. The SEC mandate has had unintentional impacts. The idea was to lower the cost of transactions for smaller investors and individuals, but it inadvertently reduced trading margins for big dealers to the point where many left the industry or reduced their market presence. The remaining participants were forced to quickly adopt electronic order management systems and more efficient routing technology. The emergence of electronic trading networks and new sophisticated trading systems further diminished profitability through lower trading costs. Decimalization and the availability of FIX are the two drivers that have promoted algorithmic trading along with the reduction of soft dollar commissions buy-side firms are willing to pay. The Financial Information Exchange (FIX) Protocol is a series of messaging specifications for electronic communication protocol developed for international real-time exchange of securities transactions in the finance markets. It has been developed through the collaboration of banks, broker-dealers, exchanges, industry utilities institutional investors, and information technology providers from around the world. A company called FIX Protocol, Ltd., established for this purpose, maintains and owns the specification, while keeping it in the public domain. FIX is open and free, but it is not software. FIX is a specification around which software developers can create commercial or open-source software, as they see fit. As the market's leading trade communications protocol, FIX is integral to many order management and trading systems. Eric Goldberg, CEO of Portware, a global securities industry's leading developer of broker-neutral trading software states, "FIX as a standardized protocol has made it possible for independent software vendors to provide destination-neutral systems for electronic trading. As the proliferation of FIX continues to increase the use of electronic trading worldwide, algorithmic trading won't be far behind. As use of FIX grows, so will the use of algorithmic trading."[1] FIX was first developed at Salomon Brothers in 1992 to facilitate equity trading between Fidelity Investments.[2] It has become the messaging standard for pre-trade and trade communication globally. This communication is done through electronic communication networks (ECNs), which use Web-based platforms. This collects limit and market orders and matches them or displays them on an Internet-based order book. The largest ECN, Instinet, was estimated to represent 12% of the trading volume on NASDAQ in February 2002, while Island, another Web-based transparent limit order book, amounted to 9.6%, RediBook 6.5%, and Archipelago 10.5%.[3] ECNs compete with traditional NASDAQ market makers, but do not take on proprietary positions. They simply handle and display customer orders. They also cannot conduct trades away from the current best market price and must allocate orders according to price priority. Decimal pricing decreased the volume of stocks that had been available at prices that were fractions of a dollar into smaller pools available at prices that differ by just a penny. Algorithmic trading has become a solution for the problem of smaller spreads and market fragmentation. Algorithmic programs have the ability to slice parent orders, which are large blocks of shares, efficiently, ensuring that each tiny order or child order gets the best price. The emergence of new niche players in the algorithmic market has created variety among market makers but does not seem to pose a serious threat to bigger Wall Street broker-dealers. There will

---

[1] Eric Goldberg, "Algorithm Panel Q&A," *FIXGlobal* 1, no. 4 (2004): 10.
[2] Wikipedia contributors, s.v. "FIX protocol," *Wikipedia, The Free Encyclopedia*, http://en.wikipedia.org/w/index.php?title=FIX_protocol&oldid=94663821 (accessed February 6, 2007).
[3] Bruno Biais, Christophe Bisiere, and Chester Spatt, "Imperfect Competition in Financial Markets: Island vs. NASDAQ," 14th Annual Utah Winter Finance Conference, AFA/EFA, November 16, 2003. Abstract. http://ssrn.com/abstract=302398 or DOI 10.2139/ssrn.302398.

always be niche players, but noncompetitive market makers are likely to step aside, while the better ones will form alliances or be acquired by larger participants. Algorithmic trading may not replace traders; it is only as effective as the traders who design and use it. However, traders who learn to use algorithmic programs more effectively will theoretically replace a large number of traders who do not understand how to use the new technologically advanced resources to their advantage. There are currently many execution choices available to traders. Some require greater human intervention and complexity; others can be automated and less complex. Each option has its drawbacks depending on the nature of a particular trade. Algorithmic trading currently focuses on equity markets but frontiers such as small cap stock have not been tapped yet. In the future, these could include fixed income, futures, options, and foreign exchange. Whether or not algorithms can work effectively with illiquid securities such as small cap stock and many fixed income instruments remains to be seen. Algorithms, which were traditionally associated with one particular asset class, namely equities, are diversifying into other markets that are rapidly evolving toward electronic trading. Participants in other asset classes such as derivatives tend to be comfortable and savvy with technology to begin with, so moving to a more systematic algorithmic approach to some of these classes may not seem as radical. Algorithmic trading has already been employed in foreign exchange markets and may soon find a place in futures and options as well. According to Sean Gilman, CTO at Currenex, "Algorithmic trading models can be thought of as "packets of strategy," individually conceived and customized to help the trader execute trading tactics with the flexibility to revise strategies swiftly or implement new ones on the fly. They allow both the sell-side and buy-side to take on a greater volume of trades with more efficiency and reduced chance for error." Fixed income instruments are most likely to be the last asset class to move in algorithmic trading. However, this technologically advanced strategy is offered in small quantities or to very liquid markets in fixed income such as U.S. treasuries and other government securities.

1.3 The Participants

Sell-side brokerage firms originally developed algorithmic programs to execute transactions on behalf of their firm's proprietary accounts. They were originally designed in-house, but outside vendors provide direct market access/order management systems for customer trading and provide a centralized order processing and clearing system. Sell-side players constantly innovate and customize their algorithms to be more competitive than their peers to offer more efficient order flow while further lowering transaction costs. They also offer their in-house algorithms to clients and smaller firms.

Algorithmic strategies offered by sell-side firms to clients are often customized, with customers having the ability to create their own stylized versions. The increase in options for customized algorithms can better serve portfolio managers' trading styles. Customized algorithms for buy-side clients can be appealing, but the wealth of options can complicate the client's ability to make the most appropriate selection, and measuring performance between different algorithms can become a daunting task. A proposed algorithmic trade should give you a visual representation of the impact cost and volatility. Post-trade data reports can theoretically guide clients with quickly available data regarding how efficiently trades have been executed. Measuring performance is crucial but often gets difficult and complex with customized order flow.

Big brokerage firms are not the only participants offering algorithm strategies; agency brokers and other vendors are providing these services to clients (see Exhibit 1.1). Algorithms are increasingly becoming more complex with average execution size decreasing to a few hundred shares from several thousand five years ago. Big brokerage firms are losing trading commissions by offering algorithms to fund managers, but they have no choice because of intense competition to lower execution costs. The role of the sales trader at brokerage firms will also change. Sell-side traders will increasingly offer consulting services advising how clients should get the best execution depending on market conditions as opposed to their traditional role of providing the execution service themselves.

The customers who use algorithmic strategies are institutions such as mutual funds, pension funds, and private money managers called hedge funds. Hedge funds are private investment firms that have fairly unrestricted investment criteria. Unlike most mutual funds, hedge funds can invest in a wide selection of investments, as well as sell-short investment products. Advances in technology and regulation-driven changes in market structure have transformed the kinds of trading options available to ensure the best execution for institutional investors. After years sitting on the sidelines, these institutions, also known as the buy side, have finally entered the algorithmic trading game. The latest advance in electronic tools allows users of algorithmic trading strategies

Market Share Algorithmic Trading Service Providers

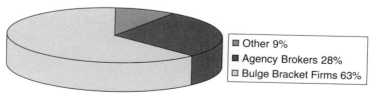

☐ Other 9%
■ Agency Brokers 28%
☐ Bulge Bracket Firms 63%

Exhibit 1.1 *Source: Algorithmic Trading Hype or Reality,* Aite Group 2005.

to predefine rules regarding how an order should be executed. Traders must calibrate the algorithms to suit their portfolio strategy. Buy-side firms such as Putnam Investments, the mutual fund giant that manages about $200 billion in assets, have used algorithms for the past couple of years. Approximately 5% of trades placed by money managers are currently executed with an in-house algorithm. This number is expected to increase to over 20% in the next couple of years. Algorithms are a step up from the more familiar program trading and pose dangers for inexperienced hedge and mutual fund traders. Algorithmic trading strategies can become predictable and display patterns. Regulators are aware of the potential problems in algorithmic trading. The NASD is currently cooperating with the Securities and Exchange Commission (SEC), collecting documents and interviewing traders to learn more about the programs and their potential for abuse. Many buy-side institutions are building their own algorithms or are considering it in the near future.

Algorithmic trading usually increases message traffic on the exchanges by adjusting and readjusting orders. According to information provided by NASDAQ, message traffic has doubled in the last year and is up more than threefold since the beginning of 2004 to the end of 2005. A significant part of electronic trading is being carried out via an algorithm or program. Program trading currently accounts for more than 50% of trading on the New York Stock Exchange. This figure is bound to climb as more fund managers trade stocks in baskets because trading algorithms allow them to do so with greater ease.

1.4 The Impact of Decimalization

The NASDAQ Stock Market implemented decimalization in 2001. The change was intended to lower trading costs and make stock prices easier to understand for investors and was proposed by Congress in the Common Cents Pricing Act of 1997, which was later mandated by the Securities and Exchange Commission Order 34-42360 in January2000. Since 1997, U.S. markets were the only major stock markets in the world that utilized fraction prices and quotes. The introduction of decimalization was executed in three phases in order to respect either capacity or market quality considerations and cause minimal disruption in financial markets:

1. **Phase I**   On March 12, 2001, 14 non–NASDAQ 100 securities were decimalized.
2. **Phase II**   On March 26, 2001, another 197 securities representing 174 companies were decimalized.
3. **Phase III**   All remaining NASDAQ securities were converted to penny increments on April 9, 2001.

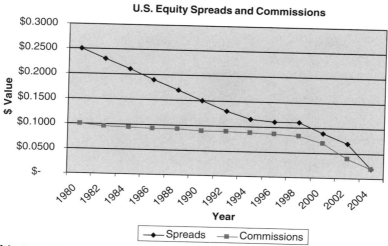

Exhibit 1.2   *Source: Institutional Equity Trading in America,* TABB Group, June 2005.

Decimalization lowered trading costs particularly for retail investors by allowing tighter bid-ask spreads (see Exhibit 1.2); however, this also resulted in significantly reduced profit for market makers, and the exit of many of those participants. According to the NASDAQ decimalization report to the SEC, for most actively traded securities, the quoted spread fell from 6.6 cents to 1.9 cents when penny increments were introduced. Among the major concerns with trading smaller tick size is the capacity impact on message traffic. The two general classes of messages that were mainly considered include quote updates disseminated by the various market centers, and the Last Sale trade report disseminated by NASDAQ.

With the introduction of decimalization, large institutional orders will most likely be broken down into smaller order flow (see Exhibit 1.3). Buy-side traders have two options to execute orders. They may direct their orders through an institutional broker working on a sales desk, having their market maker fill the order for them, or place the orders themselves through an Electronic Communication Network. The reaction from institutional investors regarding trade executions done with the decimal system has been mixed. Some buy-side traders believe there have been no increases in volume-weighted execution price, no changes in market makers' capital commitment, and no need to break up orders into smaller pieces. Other traders believe the benefits of decimalization are harder to

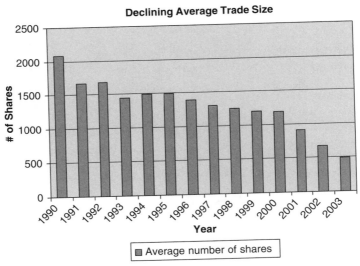

Exhibit 1.3   *Source:* NYSE.

see. They believe it has become more labor-intensive for brokers to work a large order and it takes them longer to print back trades to the buy side, so ticket costs for institutional brokers may have gone up. Finally, the possible shift to a commissioned-based model from the net-price model on various NASDAQ institutional trading desks could make it much easier for buy-side traders to track their orders' execution quality; commissions will be explicit.

1.5 The Different Faces of Electronic Trading

The definition of program and algorithmic trades is often confused and misunderstood. Terms such as "program trading," "algorithmic trading," and "black box trading" are often used interchangeably. The New York Stock Exchange defines program trading as "equity securities that encompass a wide range of portfolio-trading strategy involving the purchase or sale of a basket of at least 15 stocks valued at $1 million or more." Program trades only expedite the trade flow process, but people actually implement the trading decisions. Program trading has often been associated with three core trading strategies:

1. **Duration averaging** A strategy usually implemented when prices of a stock portfolio trade within a particular price range. A price band is put in place, which may reduce the effect of price volatility through

minimizing loss during market downturns, at the cost of maximizing profit when the market is strong.

2. **Portfolio insurance or dynamic hedging**   Works like a put option. Its objective is to insure a minimum value for a stock portfolio in a falling market. For example, a portfolio insurer might buy a put option on a particular index at a predetermined price level. If the index falls below that level, the insurer exercises or sells the put. The profit on the put offsets the decline in the value of the stocks the insurer holds. If the stocks in the index rise, the insurer loses what he paid for the put.

3. **Index arbitrage**   Involves the correlation between the stock market and the futures and options markets. Financial products sold in the futures and options markets are derived from an underlying cash product. For reasons that are inexplicable, sometimes when good news occurs, the futures and options markets for an index such as the S&P 500 are not at equilibrium with the underlying stock prices and trade above in relation to the actual market. An example of an index arbitrage opportunity would be selling expensive futures and options that are trading exuberantly but will soon return to fair valuations, and buying underlying stocks currently undervalued.

Algorithmic trading is defined as "placing a buy or sell order of a defined quantity into a quantitative model that automatically generates the timing of orders and the size of orders based on goals specified by the parameters and constraints of the algorithm."[4] The term is imprecise and ambiguous. Any trader following a set protocol could be said to have an algorithmic strategy. Algorithms are derived from the surname of famed mathematician Abu Abdullah Muhammad Musa al-Khwarizmi, who lived around 780 to 850 AD and introduced the concept of algorithms into European mathematics. Quantitative strategies by their very nature employ algorithms to search the market for trading opportunities.[5] Algorithmic trading refers to trading strategies that involve a number of simultaneous transactions, often combined according to a specific set of rules.[6] The purpose of algorithmic trading is to efficiently facilitate the size and timing of orders based on preset parameters. An example of such algorithms would be a pair of trading algorithms where two comparable securities are mispriced but expected to converge on a same price target based on their fundamental similarity. Institutions have used technology to split up large market order flow into smaller ones using algorithmic trading. This process gives traders the ability

[4] The TowerGroup, s.v. "Algorithmic Trading," *Glossary of Terms,* http://www.towergroup .com/research/content/glossary.jsp?page=1&glossaryId=382.

[5] Josh Friedlander, "Algo Wars," *Investment Dealers' Digest,* May 30, 2005: 6–8.

[6] Ibid.

to get large orders completed without moving the market. The breakdown of large orders into smaller ones takes excess liquidity or creates deficient liquidity to the market in order to minimize trading cost. In addition to algorithmic trading strategies, investors are developing trading models that analyze market data seeking predetermined opportunity patterns, and generate orders to capture those opportunities also known as "black box" trading models. Black box is a term for any system that takes orders and breaks them down into smaller ones. Black box trading tends to mean trades executed by a computer that has taken in certain market data and decides which stocks to buy or sell, typically when and how much.

There are five basic algorithms in wide use that measure the success of a trade:

1. Volume-weighted average price (VWAP)
2. Time-weighted average price (TWAP) or time slicing
3. Implementation shortfall or arrival price
4. Volume participation
5. Smart routing methods

1.6 Program Trading and the Stock Market Crash of 1987

Program trading has been the subject of considerable controversy in recent years. During the 1980s, program trading became a popular culprit whenever stock prices moved quickly, especially during sharp downturns. Initially, the stock market crash of 1987 was thought to be caused solely by program trading. Even experts at the Securities and Exchange Commission initially thought this was the case. Today, most financial economists will agree that this theory is well overblown and more than one factor affected the stock market crash of 1987.

On Monday, October 19, 1987, the Dow Jones Industrial Average fell 508.32 points and closed at a record low of 1,738.40 points. On that day, the Standard and Poor's 500 Index fell 20%, the largest decline ever recorded, eclipsing the 12% decline on Monday, October 29, 1929, which signaled the Great Depression. Program trading was quickly blamed for the declines, but program traders who were selling stock during the market downturn were clearly doing so to arbitrage their positions against declines in index futures. It is difficult to place the blame for the crash of 1987 on program trading since stock quotes were changing so rapidly on Black Monday that program trading could not have occurred because the market information needed to make transactions was continuously being updated.

The sudden drastic downturn that day does not seem to have been caused by any fundamental news about the economy either in the United States or abroad. Many industry experts place the blame on portfolio insurance. Portfolio insurers sold that day with almost no offsetting purchases. They also made matters worse by opening that day with an overhang of unexecuted sell orders from the accelerating decline of the previous week, deepening the backlog. Whenever the market seemed to rally that day, large sell orders trying to catch up with demand would suppress them. Some professional traders who were not portfolio insurers also anticipated pent-up selling demand and sold in advance; other investors may have misinterpreted the sell-off as a message being conveyed as fundamentally negative news about the market was to be announced. Investors who were unaware of portfolio insurance did not realize that portfolio insurance trades were simply responsive to previous market moves and contained no fundamental information. The other possible alternative may include investors' increased perception of stock market risk. For some unspecified reason, the risk of equity investing rose dramatically in the weeks leading up to the crash. Risk-averse investors began fleeing equities in favor of bonds. Overvalued stocks were lowered until the price of stocks reached the point where it provided adequate returns to compensate for added risk. This is sometimes called risk effect. The S&P 500 index experienced a 10% decline in the three trading days leading up to the crash, while volatility increased substantially during that month. During market declines reduced wealth leads to greater risk aversion. When negative news hits the market, driving prices down, investors respond with greater sales than before and vice versa. This is sometimes referred to as wealth effect. The correlation between individual stocks also probably rose during the market downturn, increasing risk and risk aversion and reducing the benefits of diversification. Investors also commonly rely on market liquidity to permit them to sell their positions and reduce exposure to risk. However, during the October market crash, bid-ask spreads and market impact in trading equities increased dramatically to the point where trading in many important stocks halted altogether.[7]

In conclusion, there are four economic reasons why stock market declines and increases together during high volatility:

1. **Risk effect**   Higher volatility leading to greater risk, which is implemented in the market by reducing equity prices.
2. **Wealth effect**   Lower price levels reduce wealth, which in turn increases risk aversion, which in turn leads to higher volatility.

---

[7] Mark Rubenstein, *Comments on the 1987 Stock Market Crash: Eleven Years Later,* in *Risks in Accumulation Products,* Society of Actuaries, 2000: 1–6.

3. **Diversification effect**   Correlation increases in market declines, which increases volatility and reduces opportunities for diversification.
4. **Liquidity effect**   Liquidity disappears in volatile markets, encouraging especially risk-averse traders to sell even at substantially reduced prices.

Since the crash of 1987, major stock and commodities exchanges have instituted procedures to limit mass or panic selling in times of serious market declines and volatility through implementing circuit breakers. These mechanisms are also known as the collar rule, or price limits. Circuit breakers determine whether or not trading will be halted temporarily or stopped entirely. The securities and futures markets have circuit breakers that provide for brief, coordinated cross-market trading halts during a severe market decline as measured by a single-day decrease in the Dow Jones Industrial Average (DJIA). There are three circuit breaker thresholds— 10%, 20%, and 30%—set by the markets at point levels that are calculated at the beginning of each quarter. Under NYSE Rule 80A, if the DJIA moves up or down 2% from the previous closing value, program trading orders to buy or sell the Standard & Poor's 500 stocks as part of index arbitrage strategies must be entered with directions to have the order executions effected in a manner that stabilizes share prices. The collar restrictions are lifted if the DJIA returns to or within 1% of its previous closing value. The futures exchanges set the price limits that aim to lessen sharp price swings in contracts, such as stock index futures. A price limit does not stop trading in the futures, but prohibits trading at prices below the preset limit during a price decline. Intraday price limits are removed when preset times during the trading session, such as 10 minutes after the threshold, are reached. Daily price limits remain in effect for the entire trading session. Specific price limits are set by the exchanges for each stock index futures contract. There are no price limits for U.S. stock index options, equity options, or stocks.[8]

Circuit breakers were put into place in 1988 in order to keep any future markets from dropping relentlessly in a market downturn. Many critics believe circuit breakers increase volatility instead of reducing it. There are three stages in the establishment of the circuit breaker device. The first two stages are referred to as collars. The plan is to limit computer program trading from sending orders to the New York Stock Exchange if the Dow has risen or fallen more than 50 points from the earlier day's close. The second stage of the circuit breaker plan is to postpone program trading for 5 minutes if the Dow loses 96 points and the Standard & Poor's 500 stock

[8] U.S. Securities and Exchange Commission, "Circuit Breakers and Other Market Volatility Procedures," July 29, 2005, http://www.sec.gov/answers/circuit.htm.

index drops by more than 12 points. This stage restricts traders using computer programs to make large orders. The third circuit breaker phase was designed to sever trading in all U.S. major exchanges for an hour if the Dow fell 250 points in a day. The trading would then continue after the hour had expired, but if the Dow continued to fall 150 points after trading continued, the market would then close for two more hours. Circuit breakers were installed primarily to prevent extreme changes in the stock market. Their usefulness is often in doubt because in order to prevent extreme shifts in the market, the causes of values changed must be revealed.

1.7 Conclusion

Simple algorithmic trading systems feed the market by slicing up large block orders into a hundred smaller orders. These trades slowly enter into the market over some predetermined period of time. Today's advanced trading technology can cover their tracks varying the amount they sell, and sometimes even buying back the very stock they are trying to get rid of. Algorithmic trading technology can get sophisticated; most of them are based on volume-weighted average price models. These models set buying or selling prices based on what is calculated to be the average price for a given day, in other words, they use a low-risk, follow-the-herd approach. This has its uses: it can, for example, be useful to unload a large number of shares far more quickly than might be practical manually.

In order for investors and market makers to make money, riskier strategies must be implemented to outdo their competitors, or traders must use more sophisticated algorithms than their peers. A pure alpha-seeking strategy is very underdeveloped in algorithmic trading because it is very difficult to accomplish. In this regard, human traders making the final execution decisions still have a decided advantage over pure algorithmic or program trading. The FIX Protocol has allowed different proprietary systems to plug into a common standard and communicate with one another. Some trading programs are designed to decide which shares to buy and sell. These are used for statistical arbitrage, the practice of monitoring and comparing share prices to identify patterns that can be exploited to make a profit. Some exchanges now regulate the use of electronic and algorithmic trading, preventing their systems from being overloaded or to avoid repeating the crash of 1987. On July 7, 2005, the London Stock Exchange asked for algorithmic trading to be suspended after the London bombings.

We are still in the infancy of algorithmic trading. Its impact on the corporate world is still uncertain. Algorithmic trading is now predominantly used to trade large capitalization companies, by making it easier to buy and sell large blocks of stock. It is a less well-suited means to trade small-cap or illiquid securities. The growing use of algorithmic trading could potentially lead brokers to further ignore the small-cap universe. This would result in an even further hit on smaller companies struggling to make markets to the public despite diminished stock research coverage and increased regulatory costs. At the moment, big strategic decisions such as which shares to buy or sell are made by human traders; algorithmic programs are then given the power to decide how to buy or sell shares, with the aim of hiding the client's intentions. Executing algorithms are designed to be stealthy and create as little volatility as possible. The fact that they are designed to reduce the market impact of trades should in fact have a stabilizing effect in equity markets. Some day, advances in natural language processing and statistical analysis might lead to algorithms capable of analyzing news feeds, deciding which shares to buy and sell, and devising their own strategies. Broker dealers, software vendors, and now investment institutions are entering the algorithmic arms race. Since there are so many possible trading strategies, it is doubtful that there will turn out to be one single trading algorithm that outperforms all others.

Chapter 2

Automating Trade and Order Flow

2.1 Introduction

Investment firms and broker-dealers have developed their own trading processes honed over time. Input from auditors, regulators, experience, and management have all had an influence in shaping the landscape for trade flow. Securities clearance and settlements also play a major component. It is important to balance risk, soundness, efficiency, and acceptable cost to link the process together. Technology solutions in the front and back office must be run in tandem, in terms of development rate and integration.

The financial industry has been proactively involved with the automation of trade processing. The processing environment is segregated among three subsets: pre-trade, trade, and post-trade (see Exhibit 2.1). In the post-trade sector, a vast number of nonprofessional staff are needed to process repetitive, data-intensive trade information. The personnel expense alone justifies the move to automation. Pre-trade activities have benefited immensely from the introduction of technology. Complex analytical work performed by asset managers and traders today was very difficult prior to the introduction of cost-efficient databases and high-speed computational capacity.

When a trade is traditionally executed in an exchange or in an OTC market, a number of stages must be followed in order to achieve an effective transfer of securities versus payment between counterparties. Close cooperation must exist between the front and back office to prevent mistakes. The segregation between

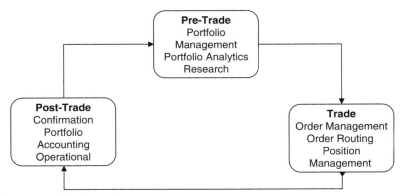

Exhibit 2.1　Trade cycle activities.

front- and back-office duties minimizes legal violations, such as fraud and embezzlement, or violation of regulations. Operational integrity is maintained through the independent processing of trades, trade confirmations, and settlements. The back office serves several vital functions. It records and confirms trades transacted and provides internal control mechanisms segregating duties. A properly functioning back office will help ensure the integrity of the financial institution and minimize operations, settlement, and legal risks.

The links between front- and back-office operations may range from totally manual to fully computerized systems. The complexity of linking systems should be related to the volume of trading activities undertaken. Operational risk is the risk that information systems or internal controls result in unexpected loss. It can be monitored through examining a series of plausible scenarios. It can be assessed through reviews of procedures, data processing systems, and other operating practices.

2.2　Internal Controls

Formal written procedures should be in place for purchase, sales, processing, accounting, clearance, and activities related to transactions. These procedures should be designed to ensure that financial contracts are properly recorded and senior management is aware of exposure, gains, or losses resulting from trading activities. Desirable controls include[1]

1. written documentation indicating the range of permissible products, trading authorities, and permissible counterparties;

---

[1] Mario Guadamillas and Robert Keppler, "Securities Clearance and Operations Systems: A Guide to Best Practices," World Bank 2003: 19–24.

2. written position limits for each type of contract or risk type;
3. a market risk management system to monitor the organization's exposure to market risk, and written procedures for authorizing trades and excess of position limits;
4. a credit risk management system to monitor the organization's exposure to customers and broker dealers;
5. separation of duties and supervision to ensure that persons executing transactions are not involved in approving the accounting methodology or entries;
6. a clearly defined flow of order tickets and confirmations designed to verify accuracy and enable reconciliations throughout the system and to enable the reconcilement of trader's position reports to those positions maintained by an operating unit;
7. procedures for promptly resolving failures to receive or deliver securities on the date securities are settled;
8. guidelines for the appropriate behavior of dealing and controlling staff and training of competent personnel to follow written policies and guidelines.

2.3 Trade Cycle

Once a transaction has been executed by the front office, the trade-processing responsibility rests with various back-office personnel. The back office is responsible for processing all payments and delivery or receipt of securities, commodities, and written contracts. They are responsible for verifying the amounts and direction of payments that are made under a range of netting agreements.

Trade processing involves entering a trade agreement on the correct form or into an automated system. After the front office has inputted the trade, verification of transaction data should be performed. Copies of the trade agreement are used for bookkeeping entries and settlements. It is appropriate to evaluate whether an institution's automated trade-processing system provides adequate support for its processing functions.

CONFIRMATIONS

When a transaction is agreed upon, a confirmation is sent to the counterparty. The back office should then initiate, follow up, and control counterparty confirmations. A strictly controlled confirmation process helps to prevent fraudulent trades. For example, a trader may enter into a fraudulent deal, or a trader could enter into a contract, send the original confirmation, and then destroy copies. This may allow the trader to build up positions without the knowledge of management. The trader when closing out the position would make up a ticket for the originally destroyed contract and pass it on together with the offsetting contract so that the position is netted off. Receipt and verification of incoming confirmations by an independent department would immediately uncover this type of activity.

SETTLEMENT PROCESS

After a purchase or sale has been made, the transaction must be cleared through back-office interaction with a clearing agent. On the settlement date, payments or instruments are exchanged and general ledger entries are updated. Settlement is completed when the buyer or buyer's agent has received or delivered securities and the seller has been paid. Brokers may assign these tasks to a separate organization such as a clearinghouse, but remain responsible to their customers for ensuring the transactions were handled properly. Losses may be incurred if the counterparty fails to make delivery. In some cases, the clearing agent and broker are liable for any problems that occur in completing the transaction. Settlement risk should be controlled through the continuous monitoring of movement of the institution's money and securities by the establishment of counterparty limits by the credit department.

RECONCILIATION

The back office should perform timely reconciliation with the policies and procedures of the institution. The individual responsible for performing the reconcilement of accounts should be independent of the person responsible for the input of transaction data. Reconciliation should determine positions held by the front office, as well as provide an audit trail for regulatory reporting. The typical reports that need to be reconciled include trader positions, regulatory reports, broker statements, and income statements.

THE EVOLUTION OF TRADE FLOW

Today's front office has focused primarily on automation and technology. Trade confirmation and matching have seriously lagged behind. Firms have leveraged technology to remain competitive in the face of rising costs, tighter margins, greater regulation, and compliance. The rise of electronic and algorithmic trading is the clearest representation of this through the influence of complex technology and trading strategies. Regulation has increased pressure on costs. Market conditions, increased competition, and more educated investors have all put pressure on the securities industry to focus on the bottom line and cope with squeezes in margin. As a result of these changes, the back office has lagged behind. There are a number of trends, however, that are helping the back office come up to speed. First, is the adoption of back-office outsourcing, by both traditional investment managers to banks and hedge funds. Outsourcing trends are allowing investment firms to concentrate on their core business, while improving operational efficiency.

2.4 Straight-Through Processing and Trade Automation

The advancement of back-office automation and the use of computer technology to analyze and record trade history have led to the evolution of pre-trade analytics and processes. An increasing amount of market information became available. Bloomberg was a pioneer in this area, merging market data with security information and analytics. These advances allowed information management opportunities to arise between the back and front office. Firms began to devise a means to integrate data flow between two previously distinct sectors of an organization, yielding advances toward straight-through processing (STP).

Efforts have been under way to redirect capital investment toward advances in liquidity, efficiency, and market transparency through the application of technology. The equity and foreign exchange markets have benefited most to date. Open access to historical trade information has been emphasized by the Securities and Exchange Commission (SEC). Institutional money managers continue to control growing proportions of the world's financial assets. This has caused greater pressure on traditional market structures to provide open, equal access to trading venues for all market participants. Broker-dealers have been faced with challenges as well. Heavy competition has forced dealers to invest a great deal in the automation of existing market processes. These investments are yielding diminishing value as time progresses, leading to the conclusion that market structures will have to change to continue providing gains. Ultimately, shifting to more efficient markets has become a common goal for all market participants.

STRAIGHT-THROUGH PROCESSING

The most tangible and immediate gain in expanding automation in market transactions is through the use of scalable STP. The benefits of STP include reduced settlement costs and short intervals between trade date and settlement date. Connectivity to trading partners through a common protocol will allow much progress toward these goals. Other benefits of STP include speed of information flow, allowing shorter settlement times. The second is the consistency of electronic data achieved when manual manipulation of that data is kept to a minimum. Pre-trade activities have been automated through the use of technology. Market participants practice pre-trade modeling, analytics, and position management. In most cases, the data being manipulated in this environment has been entered electronically from post-trade systems.

Today, trading is accomplished through a combination of electronic and face-to-face telephone interaction. Trading environments are often so fast paced that information can be incorrectly relayed and interpreted. Information is often not inputted at the time of trade and data can be lost, misinterpreted, or entered incorrectly. The greatest gain of STP is shortened settlement periods. However, settling daily trading activity through a shortened time frame can become a daunting task. Electronic trading can potentially eliminate many of these problems. Data will theoretically be consistent since orders will be created using integrated systems.

A key technological development that has resulted from electronic trading and STP is the development of algorithmic trading. The components of algorithmic trading can be broken down into four pieces: data management, strategy enabler, order management systems, and order routing.[2]

2.5 Data Management

Historical and real-time data has become a clear competitive advantage in a business highly dependent on programs, algorithms, and other black box mechanisms used to achieve the best execution. Automated electronic trading models can execute tens of thousands of trades per day, becoming a prevalent strategy among both buy-side and sell-side traders. The emergence of advanced electronic trading, which hinges on real-time analysis of market information, will force firms to aggressively improve their data infrastructure. In an all-electronic market, speed to market is a competitive advantage. Firms need to measure their trading environment through tracking capacity, latency, execution quality, and a host of other metrics necessary to hone their execution process. Accurately measuring a firm's operations enables them to provide better service, better manage costs, and reduce operational friction. Many sell-side firms have been implementing real-time measuring

---

[2] Sang Lee, "Algorithmic Trading: Hype or Reality?" Aite Group Report 20050328, March 2005: 20.

and monitoring of algorithmic trading. They constantly measure the performance of the algorithm versus the goal and watching the back-end processes, which include fill rates, executions, performance trajectories, and the limit orders entering the market. They track order routing systems measuring how long it takes to generate the proposed trajectory and get the first order to the market. When a problem is spotted, such as a stuck order, a lost fill, a misaligned model trajectory, or slackening in performance, the algorithm can be recalibrated quickly.

Strategy Enablers

Clients use databases and analytic tools as a foundation for analyzing massive amounts of data to develop new and existing algorithms. These platforms are configured for developing pre- and post-trade analytics of real-time historical data. Examples of where analytical and historical data can help make trading decisions include directed order flow, blocking and netting, liquidity characteristics, low-value added executions, high-value executions, and transaction cost analysis.

Traders need to determine where orders are directed, taking into account best execution responsibilities and transaction costs. The directed orders should be analyzed, and often traders desire research and trading ideas from brokers. Broker research is still highly valued for trading ideas and implementing strategy. Specified use of trading cost is allocated to research-supplying brokers. Large money managers value broker research. The vast number of industries, companies, products, and trends make it impossible for investors to follow everything internally. According to the TABB Group, more than 90% of larger firms value research (see Exhibit 2.2) despite the fact that over the past few years, there has been increasing scrutiny over how firms pay for this research. The majority of research and most investment-related expenditures were paid for with soft dollars. Soft dollars are commission payment agreements between brokers and their investment management clients to fund research and investment-related services. Soft dollars enable the money manager to compensate the broker for the value of research tied in to transaction costs.

After an order is directed, traders need to route orders that need to be blocked or netted with other orders of the same security and execution instructions. After the order is netted or blocked and routed, the trader needs to add value to the trade. This is done by analyzing the security to decide if the trade can be executed better than the current market. This is usually maximized when spreads are larger, the liquidity lower, and the size of the trade is greater. The payback on the trader's time is greater in individually managing the execution.

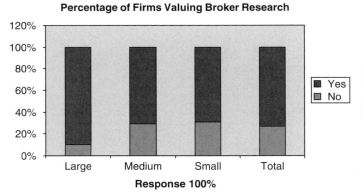

Exhibit 2.2   *Source: Institutional Equity Trading in America,* TABB Group, June 2005.

As algorithmic trading becomes mainstream, traders will need to allocate soft dollar commitments, trading relationships, best execution concerns, algorithmic functionality, and trader intuition. When markets are efficient, with strong liquidity, this creates a situation of low value-added executions. A balance must be met in terms of routing orders to brokers who provide research with outstanding soft dollars committed, as opposed to routing orders through an algorithmic trading model that will execute the order in relation to an investor's trading strategy. When spreads are wide, and liquidity low, traders think about taking more control of the execution. Traders are in a situation with high value-added execution scenario. Many firms use ECNs but they should also think seriously about aggregate platforms as well. Aggregation looks at the market agnostically, to provide smart order routing, enable traders to more selectively manage their execution, and provide consistent order types and order management facilities, which enable them to better control their trading environment.

Transaction cost analysis (TCA) will become more integrated into the trading process. As TCA models increase in sophistication with order management and portfolio management technologies become more tightly integrated, investment managers and hedge funds will use TCA more extensively to monitor their trading effectiveness.

2.6 Order Management Systems

Order management systems (OMS) evolved as traders require better tools to manage workflow in an execution environment. The OMS collects orders

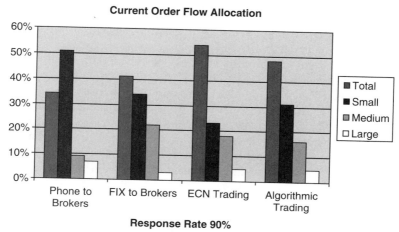

Exhibit 2.3 *Source: Institutional Equity Trading in America,* TABB Group, April 2004.

and instructions from various portfolio managers, aggregating them into blocks, managing executions, collecting fills and performing allocations. Exhibit 2.3 presents how these orders are currently allocated and broken down by the size of the investment firm (see Exhibit 2.3).

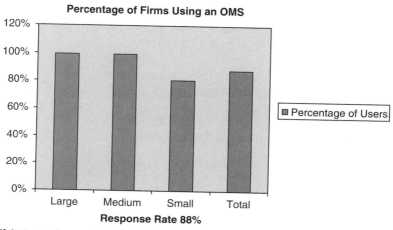

Exhibit 2.4 *Source:* TABB Group.

There are several key features in an effective order management system:

1. **Trade blotter** A trade blotter functions as the central hub, enabling traders to manage orders/lists, apply various benchmarks on the fly, and keep track of current positions, execution data, confirmations, and real-time P&L.
2. **Prepackaged algorithms** Most firms now offer prepackaged algorithms designed to attract those smaller firms that lack algorithm-building capacity. The key to prepackaged algorithms is to ensure that they are flexible enough to enable modification and customization by the clients.
3. **Pre- and post-trade analytics** Pre-trade analytics can help traders determine which algorithm is most suitable given a certain trading situation as well as estimating cost for a given trade. Post-trade analytics can be used to measure trading performance via a benchmark and other firm established trading parameters.
4. **FIX connectivity** FIX is the lifeline of algorithmic trading systems and allows buy-side traders and brokers to communicate electronically. It enables the system to make timely trading decisions driven by algorithms.
5. **Handling multiple asset classes** Algorithmic trading systems should be able to go beyond just equities in terms of financial products supported. A typical system currently handles equity, derivatives, FX, etc.
6. **Compliance and regulatory reporting** Similar to single stock/block trading, order management systems must be able to accommodate the constantly changing regulatory environment of the U.S. securities industry through customizable, rules-based compliance triggers and flexible reporting capability.[3]

The following steps list the details of a sample trade through an OMS:[4]

1. A portfolio-rebalancing algorithm recommends a buy of 300,000 shares of IBM.
2. An OMS accepts this data and displays it to the trader so they may make a decision on where to direct the trade.
3. When the trader sees they need to buy 300,000 shares of IBM, they look at an ECN aggregator, which displays the full depth of the IBM book across the multiple ECNs and exchanges.
4. The buy-side trader makes a decision on where to direct the trades in IBM. The options include:

---

[3] Sang Lee, "Algorithmic Trading: Hype or Reality?" Aite Group Report 20050328, March 2005: 16–17.

[4] Lori Master, White Paper: "ECN Aggregators—Increasing Transparency and Liquidity in Equity Markets," *Random Walk Computing*, Fall 2004: 6–8.

- Send blocks of 50,000 shares through a broker dealer to satisfy soft dollar agreements such as sell-side research, etc.
- Utilize an algorithm such as Volume-Weighted Average Price (VWAP) and let the algorithm judge the patterns, and smart routing features will search for the best firm price available at the time of each order.

5. The executing trading desks would send back the execution information to the trader's OMS. The OMS can then submit the fill data to a system such as AccessPlexus for execution quality evaluation.

2.7 Order Routing

Order routing is the domain of direct market access (DMA) technology providers. It figures out what types of orders and where to send orders in order to receive optimal execution to meet the parameters set by a trading strategy. Some of the leading DMA players are trying to differentiate themselves by expanding into other asset classes or trying to build their own OMS system. DMA is valued for its ability to bridge the fragmented liquidity or multiple marketplaces (see Exhibit 2.5); however, acquisitions by NASDAQ and the exchanges have decreased this ability to bridge gaps.

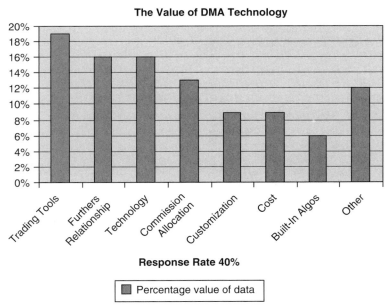

Exhibit 2.5 *Source: Institutional Equity Trading in America,* TABB Group, June 2005.

In 2005, NASDAQ acquired Brut and Instinet, and the NYSE merged with Archipelago. Markets are consolidating, reducing the need for an aggregated platform. DMA providers are expanding to become full execution platforms. These providers are looking not only to aggregate liquidity, but also to provide electronic trading tools such as algorithms, TCA, and pre-trade analytics. Several DMA platforms have also launched multi-broker models, allowing efficient distribution of soft dollars without routing order flow around the street.

2.8 Liquidity Shift

Technology providers are increasingly offering better access to route orders to make trading easier and efficient. Firms reallocate orders based on lower commissions to increase investment performance, and provide better access to liquidity. Buy-side firms are increasingly utilizing algorithms, and route less and less order flow over the phone (see Exhibit 2.6). They are diverting a larger percentage of their order flow away from sales traders toward low-touch to no-touch channels such as DMA. The role of the sales trader is evolving. As the buy side finds better ways of finding its own methods to execute trades through algorithms, or through DMAs, brokers and salespeople will need to focus on other areas that can create value. The sales trader's role can expand to helping buy-side traders determine how to customize algorithms, helping determine which models to use, and providing customization advice.

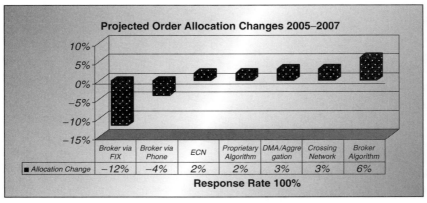

Projected Order Allocation Changes 2005–2007

	Broker via FIX	Broker via Phone	ECN	Proprietary Algorithm	DMA/Aggregation	Crossing Network	Broker Algorithm
■ Allocation Change	−12%	−4%	2%	2%	3%	3%	6%

Response Rate 100%

Exhibit 2.6 *Source: Institutional Equity Trading in America,* TABB Group, June 2005.

SELL-SIDE STRUGGLE

Investment management firms send less and less order flow to sales desks. Commission dollars have dropped over 20% in the last three years and further declines are expected. Negative sentiment toward brokers, which stems from information leakage and execution quality, creates further friction among the buy side. Investment firms are increasingly hesitant to pay commission fees to brokers while utilizing DMA platforms and independent research firms. Exhibit 2.7 displays the breakdown of the types of services which add value for the buy-side through connecting to an order management system with a broker dealer. Connecting to OMSs is becoming a requirement to do business, but it is also a steppingstone to alternative solutions for investment firms to find liquidity.

As more broker volume hits the algorithmic trading desks, the role of the sales trader will change. Brokers will shift from order takers looking for the best execution to idea providers. A new trend in services will come about, such as algorithmic trading consultants and service providers. As commission dollars continue to fall, investment managers are becoming less selective about broker relationships. Alternate research sources, along with the time and energy it requires to maintain a relationship, also contribute to the decline.

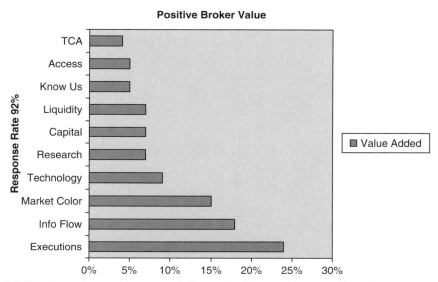

Exhibit 2.7 *Source: Institutional Equity Trading in America,* TABB Group, June 2005.

2.9 Conclusion

As the financial industry utilizes electronic trading systems more and more, ideas for enhanced functionality will continue. Technological advancement such as the Internet will allow market participants to integrate and develop more advanced trading applications. The movement of liquidity from one environment to another will happen more quickly and efficiently. Meaningful challenges are presented to existing market participants in order to remain competitive. The advancement of straight-through processing will lead to many benefits of electronic transactions. Greater market liquidity results from shorter time frames between trade and settlement. Strategically incorporating the increase of electronic executions will become the highest value for technology available to market participants today.

Chapter 3

The Growth of Program and Algorithmic Trading

3.1 Introduction

Program trading volume, also known as portfolio trading, has increased dramatically in the past several years. The NYSE reports that in 2000, 22% of all trading on the Big Board was executed via programs, up from 11.6% in 1995. In 2004, that number has increased to 50.6% (see Exhibit 3.1).

Program trades provide money managers with the ability to execute a basket of stocks without being subject to the variance of each individual stock. The portfolio can benefit from diversification, where the risk of the whole can be smaller than the risk of the sum of the parts. It gives the trader the ability to focus on controlling the market and sector risk while seeking to minimize the market impact of the whole portfolio. The greater availability of technology and the increasing use of modern portfolio techniques are driving the recent growth in program trading (see Exhibit 3.2).

In comparison to the phenomenal growth of program trading, block trading activity within the NYSE has declined rapidly, going from 56% in 1996 to approximately 30% by the end of 2004 (see Exhibit 3.3). The introduction of decimalization has had a huge negative impact on the overall block trading business for the past several years.

Traditional trades executed by the buy side have relied on "block trading." Information flow is crucial in understanding the stock's dynamics in order to make educated trading decisions. This information flow is required for

Year	Total % of Program Trades on the NYSE	% of Buy Programs on the NYSE	% of Sell Programs on the NYSE
2004	50.6%	25.8%	24.7%
2003	37.5%	19.2%	18.3%
2002	32.2%	16.8%	15.5%
2001	27.8%	14.6%	13.2%
2000	22.0%	11.3%	10.7%
1999	19.7%	9.8%	9.9%
1998	17.5%	9.0%	8.5%
1997	16.8%	8.6%	8.1%
1996	13.3%	6.9%	6.5%
1995	11.6%	6.4%	5.2%
1994	11.6%	5.3%	6.3%
1993	11.9%	6.5%	5.4%
1992	11.5%	5.8%	5.7%
1991	11.0%	5.9%	5.1%
1990	10.7%	5.2%	5.5%
1989	9.9%	5.4%	4.5%

Exhibit 3.1   NYSE program trading participation. *Source:* NYSE.

effective block trading especially for large orders and illiquid securities. Another feature of block trading is capital commitment. Large and illiquid orders often require the broker to become a principal in a transaction. The buy side is often confronted with investment decisions in which a dozen or more securities must be executed at once. As the number of different securities increases, so does the amount of information that must

Growth in Program Trading at the NYSE

Exhibit 3.2   *Source:* Aite Group, NYSE.

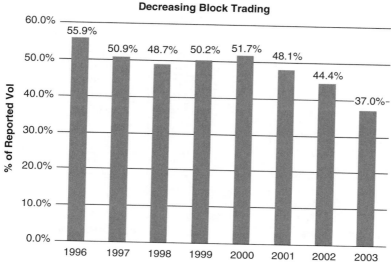

Exhibit 3.3   *Source:* Aite Group, NYSE.

be received and processed by the trader. The risk of executions increases due to the inability to process and respond to market intelligence efficiently. For example, when a trader is given the task of purchasing a list consisting of dozens of securities with no specific performance benchmark on a "best effort" execution basis, the trader is then given the tactical decision-making responsibility at his or her discretion.

3.2 A Sample Program Trade

The first step to trading a portfolio of stocks involves determining the optimal tranche size and generating pre-trade liquidity. After a trader has decided the list of stocks to trade, suitability and strategy must be analyzed. Generally speaking, a list of stocks with quantities that represent less than 35% of the average daily volume (ADV) can be suitable in a program-trading strategy. Portfolio trading is highly automated and crossing portfolios with other trade lists that contain higher or lower ADV levels is easily executable. Once a general goal is set, the trader can start to formulate a general trading strategy such as trying to achieve quality executions while minimizing market impact.

The table in Exhibit 3.4 shows the liquidity breakdown of a 300 mm portfolio. The liquidity range numbers represent a percentage of the average daily trading volume. The average daily volumes are measured over 20 days.

Liquidity Range of Average Daily Volume ADV%		Portfolio Characteristics			
Lower	Upper	Stocks	Shares	$ Value	Weight
0.0%	0.5%	100	14,498,579	300,027,060	100.00%
0.5%	2.5%	53	24,934	3,717,268	1.24%
2.5%	5.0%	38	6,545,310	162,036,173	54.01%
5.0%	10.0%	6	6,686,544	116,923,962	38.97%
10.0%	15.0%	0	687,634	15,834,422	5.28%
15.0%	20.0%	1	0	0	0.00%
20.0%	30.0%	0	554,157	1,515,236	0.51%
30.0%	40.0%	0	0	0	0.00%
40.0%	50.0%	0	0	0	0.00%
50.0%	100.0%	0	0	0	0.00%
100.0%	200.0%	0	0	0	0.00%

Exhibit 3.4   *Source:* Thomas Levy, *Program Trading: An Introduction*.

The example highlights that in this portfolio of 300 million, only 0.5% would take over 10% of a day's average volume. This portfolio is considered liquid.

One of the most prevalent benchmarks in utilizing pre-trade analysis today is the Volume-Weighted Average Price (VWAP). This is calculated by adding the dollars traded for every transaction in terms of price and multiplying that by shares traded, and then dividing that by the total shares traded for that day. VWAP is a popular measure in comparative results. This benchmark can theoretically encourage the least amount of market impact since executions are optimally distributed over the course of the day. A general VWAP strategy can limit impact by coordinating the timing of trades with intraday liquidity patterns of the stocks contained in the list. The ability to deliver high-quality executions for a large list of stocks is one reason why program trading has been more and more accepted. Cash can be easily invested by using a program trade to purchase a perfect predetermined fund weighting. Program trading also has the ability to handle the complexity that results from intraday market volatility. Large intraday swings in stock prices can make trade execution more difficult. The flexibility of a computerized program trading system provides traders with the ability to better manage risk.

CONVENIENCE AND OPPORTUNITY COST

Convenience is a major reason to utilize programs. An individual may experience difficulty in working a large list of stocks. A significant amount of time is required to individually trade a list of 50 securities consisting of a few thousand shares each. This may not be an ideal use of time considering the difficulty in the decision-making process of which securities to trade alone. The time-consuming effect of trading each security individually also has an effect on opportunity cost. There is a negative correlation between opportunity cost and trading cost as a function of time. Opportunity cost can be reduced utilizing a program trade (see Exhibit 3.5). For example, a one-sided transaction consisting of many securities has important timing advantages if executed promptly. A program trade can be done considerably faster than if done via individual block trades. The efficient use of program trading can reduce the time it takes to trade a large list of securities compared to traditional methods. The time savings can also result in lower opportunity cost, which can subsequently result in lower total cost.

3.3 The Downside of Program Trading

Today's commission costs for executing automated trades through a broker-dealer have become increasingly cheaper. When a buy-side institution obtains a quote for a "blind bid" principal program trade, the quote and commission costs are meant to price the risk associated with the broker buying or selling the program for a customer. Exhibit 3.6 shows a scenario that may potentially occur when executing a program trade.

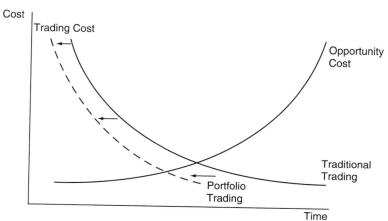

Exhibit 3.5   Trading cost and opportunity cost.

Principal Blind Bid Program Trading

How it's supposed to work	How it often works
Buy-side clients solicit bids on the program trade so that there is no leakage-based market impact	Broker can guess component stocks or highly correlated ones, based on the trade characteristic.
Strike time is meant to capture prices free of market impact. The trade is then executed at that contaminated price.	Strike time captures an adverse price that has the "imprint" of market impact from pre-hedging.
Broker's basis points (bps) quote is meant to fully compensate the broker for the risk involved in providing capital for the trade.	The broker can provide low bps quote, even a "net zero" trade because of pre-hedging.
The bps cost is a full reflection of the fees the customer pays to the broker.	The low bps cost makes the trade look like a "free lunch" but the true cost includes market impact from pre-hedging by the broker. Too often overlooked by the customer.

Exhibit 3.6   Principal blind bid program trading. *Source:* Pure Portfolio Trading Solutions, Instinet.

THE SERVICE PROVIDERS AND COMPETITORS

The key service providers for program and algorithmic service providers can be broken down by sell-side and independent third-party technology vendors:[1]

- **Bulge-bracket firms**   Large Wall Street investment banks such as Goldman Sachs, Credit Suisse, and Morgan Stanley have built reputable algorithmic trading services (see Exhibit 3.7). These firms also operate block trading desks, program trading desks, direct market access (DMA), and other trade execution services. Their ultimate goal is to facilitate order flow. These large broker-dealers look to leverage existing relationships that provide research, investment banking services, and prime brokerage to asset management firms and hedge funds.
- **Agency brokers**   Technology-driven agency brokers may either provide direct access services, and/or algorithmic trading services. Most of these firms are focused on supporting algorithmic trading as an efficient means to offer their traditional agency brokerage services.

---

[1] Sang Lee, "Algorithmic Trading: Hype or Reality?" Aite Group Report 20050328, March 2005.

Firm	Service	Representative Technology Components
Credit Suisse	Advanced Execution Services (AES)	PathFinder, proprietary
Goldman Sachs	Goldman Sachs Algorithmic Trading (GSAT)	REDIPlus, TradeFactory, The Guide
JP Morgan	Electronic Execution Services	Proprietary
Lehman Brothers	Lehman Model Execution (LMX)	LehmanLive LINKS, Portfolio WebBench
Morgan Stanley	Benchmark Execution Services	Passport, Navigator, Scorecard, EPA
Merrill Lynch	ML X-ACT	Proprietary

Exhibit 3.7 Sample of bulge-bracket firms and advanced execution services. *Source:* Aite Group.

The most established agency brokers include BNY brokerage, Instinet, and ITG (see Exhibit 3.8). Smaller agency brokers include Automated Trading Desk (ATD), Miletus Trading, Lime Brokerage, FutureTrade, UNX, and EdgeTrade.

- **Leading technology providers:**
  Data management Leading providers of data management include Xenomorph, Kx Systems, and Vhayu Technologies.
  Order Management Systems Leading algorithmic order management system vendors include Portware and FlexTrade.

Firm	Headquarters	Number of Employees	Number of Clients
BNY Brokerage	New York, NY	300+	N/A
Edge Trade	New York, NY	30	100+
Future Trade	New York, NY	105	200+
ITG	New York, NY	653	100+
Lime Brokerage	New York, NY	15	50+
Miletus Trading	New York, NY	19	40
Neonet	Stockholm, Sweden	70	145

Exhibit 3.8 Representative agency brokers. *Source:* Aite Group.

Direct market access (DMA)   Leading direct market access technology providers include Lava Trading (now part of Citigroup), Neovest, and Sonic Financial Technologies (now part of Bank of New York).

Trading networks   An important piece of the execution value chain is third-party trading networks that link trading desks with major liquidity sources as well as trading counterparties and industry utilities. Leading trading networks include STN, Radianz, Savvis, and TNS.

Analytics   External providers of pre- and post-trade analytics firms (mostly focused on post-trade data at this point) include Quantitative Services Group (QSG) and Plexus Group.

According to the Aite Group, bulge-bracket firms have dominated the marketplace in terms of market share of the algorithmic trading services market. Leading bulge-bracket firms account for over 60% of all algorithmic trading volume (both proprietary and client orders). Agency brokers represent a distant second with 28%. Other services include independent technology providers not included in agency brokers.

3.4 Market Growth and IT Spending

Most of the growth in algorithmic trading has been driven by the sell-side and hedge funds. Hedge funds are private investment vehicles that have unrestricted investment logic. While many hedge funds use traditional value and growth-based investing strategy, many use more advanced quantitative strategies, and are most likely to use cutting-edge technology such as algorithmic trading. The Aite Group estimates that at the end of 2004, approximately 25% of total equities trading volume was driven by algorithmic trading (see Exhibit 3.9). Within this 25%, the sell side was composed of 13% followed by hedge fund volume, which stood at 10% of the total. Algorithmic trading volume initiated by traditional money managers was less than 3%. The popular use of algorithmic trading by hedge funds can also be attributable to the explosive growth in hedge funds within the last 15 years (see Exhibit 3.10).

IT Spending in Algorithmic Trading

Algorithmic trading services will continue to rise. IT spending will also rise. At the end of 2004, $200 million USD was spent on different IT components that make up algorithmic trading services, according to the Aite Group. Order Management Systems accounted for over 60% of that

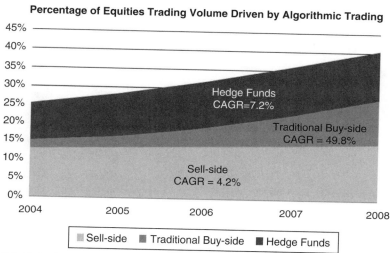

Exhibit 3.9 Percentage of equities trading volume driven by algorithmic trading. *Source:* Aite Group analysis.

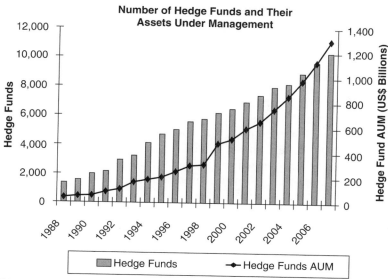

Exhibit 3.10 *Source:* Van Hedge Funds Advisors International, Aite Group analysis.

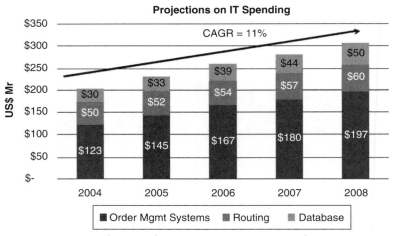

Exhibit 3.11   Projected IT spending. *Source:* Aite Group analysis.

total spending. By 2008, IT spending on algorithmic trading is expected to reach over $300 million USD (see Exhibit 3.11).

3.5 Conclusion

The growth and enhancement in pre- and post-trade analysis will play a large role in examining the performance of algorithms. The buy side will need to be increasingly educated on the usage of these tools to navigate more efficiently around the numerous algorithmic strategies at their disposal. The growth in program and algorithmic trading will depend on the cost-benefit analysis between quality of execution and the commission cost to execute a low-touch trade. The commission costs for algorithmic and direct market access trading are the lowest in the industry by far, but firms must also take into account indirect costs such as trade impact, anonymity, missed trade, and quality of execution. Equities was the first asset class to adopt algorithms. Long-term growth opportunities for program and algorithmic trades lie in fixed-income instruments, options, foreign exchange, and futures markets.

Chapter 4

Alternative Execution Venues

4.1 Introduction

The introduction of Electronic Communication Networks (ECNs), increasing pressure from institutional investors calling for better transparency, along with regulatory intervention was intended to result in superior price discovery and liquidity for routed orders. This can help facilitate more efficient order flow for program and algorithmic trades. The elimination of Rule 390 has promoted Web-based trading connecting buyers and sellers with a high-speed yet low-cost alternative. This can eliminate or reduce the effectiveness of intermediaries such as specialists and dealers. The drivers for consolidating through exchange mergers and offering alternative execution venues include the following:

- **Alternative execution venues** Large bulge-bracket firms are steering U.S. stock trades away from the exchanges routing them to their internal systems. The Aite Group estimates that share will probably increase to 18% by 2010 as more investment banks bypass the NYSE and NASDAQ. Exchanges are scrambling to compete with new technologies and cost through mergers and acquisitions.
- **Regulatory pressure** The elimination of Rule 390 and the introduction of the Order Protection rule implemented in Reg NMS, which will potentially eliminate the role of the NYSE floor broker who is currently given institutional orders to work in reserve. The Trade-Through Rule currently exists under listed exchanges but exempt NASDAQ markets. The new mandate will specify that an exchange cannot

execute an order at a worse price if a better price is available. Under the new rule, hidden reserves or better-priced orders that are not exposed will no longer be protected.

- **Cost savings** The pressure to consolidate has been driven by institutional investors attempting to squeeze costs through greater computerization, and drifting away from floor-based systems with more human intervention. ECNs have forced exchanges to upgrade their technology, consolidate through mergers, and offer better transparency to compete with other low cost execution venues.
- **Speed of execution** The recent merger activity with stock exchanges has been a result of new technologies automating trade process flow such as ECNs. This could lead to huge cost savings such as integrating two platforms, or abandoning one of the inferior electronic trading platforms.
- **Desire for anonymity** ECNs are designed to offer cost-efficient trading as well as valuable anonymity features through Web-based intermediaries.

4.2 Structure of Exchanges

The advancement of technology has changed the landscape of securities trading. This transformation began with the implementation of the Intermarket Trading System (ITS) in 1978. It was designed to disseminate trading data across the nine U.S. stock exchanges to allow market participants to choose the market that offers the best price for a given transaction. By the late 1990s, electronic communication networks, known as ECNs, which match buyers and sellers through an electronic system, emerged. This began threatening the existence of the NYSE. Prior to 1998, the NYSE had invested little or no resources in multiple equity trade matching systems. ECNs are designed to offer cost-efficient trading as well as valuable anonymity features through Web-based intermediaries. The global trend in the exchange market has been consolidation. This has not been limited to equities, but also across different asset classes in order to enable clients to trade listed and OTC equities, as well as derivative products and even fixed-income instruments. The pressure to consolidate has been driven by institutional investors attempting to squeeze costs through greater computerization, and drifting away from floor-based systems with more human intervention. Many exchanges such as the NYSE have gone public to raise money for acquisitions. The NYSE was a nonprofit entity that long benefited from the member ownership model where seat holders may have different interests from the investor (see Exhibit 4.1). The NYSE

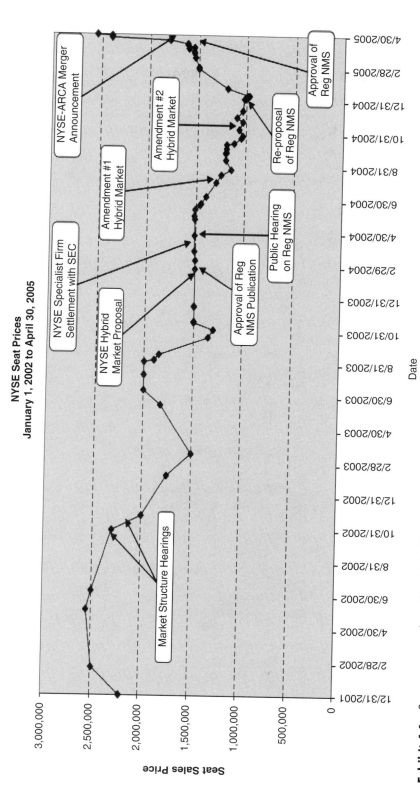

Exhibit 4.1 *Source:* sec.gov/news/speech/spch050605css-attach.pdf.

convinced its members to go public by offering shares in exchange for their membership. Now that the members have become shareholders, they have a bigger incentive to support change, such as enhancing an all-electronic operation, and mergers such as the one completed with Archipelago.

As of Q22006, the NYSE Group and NASDAQ collectively account for 78% of the entire U.S. equities market. According to the Aite Group, 20 other execution venues are battling for the remaining 22% of the U.S. equities market share (see Exhibit 4.2).

THE NYSE GROUP, INC

The NYSE Group, Inc (NYSE:NYX) operates two securities exchanges: the New York Stock Exchange (NYSE) and NYSE Arca (formerly known as the Archipelago Exchange, or ArcaEx), and the Pacific Exchange. The NYSE Group is a leading provider of securities listing, trading, and market data products and services. The NYSE is the world's largest and most liquid cash equities exchange. The NYSE provides a reliable, orderly, liquid, and efficient marketplace where investors buy and sell listed companies' stock and other securities. Listed operating companies represent a total global market capitalization of over $22.9 trillion. In the first quarter of 2006, on an average trading day, over 1.7 billion shares valued over $65 billion were traded on the NYSE.[1]

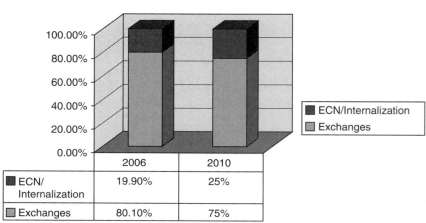

U.S. Equities Market Share Comparison

	2006	2010
ECN/ Internalization	19.90%	25%
Exchanges	80.10%	75%

Exhibit 4.2   U.S. equities market share. *Source:* Aite Group.

---

[1] The NYSE Group Inc, http://www.nyse.com/about/1088808971270.html.

4.3 Rule 390

In May 2000, Rule 390, which prohibited companies listed on the NYSE before April 1979 to engage in off-floor transactions away from a national securities exchange, was rescinded. The NYSE has defended Rule 390 on the basis that it was not intended to protect the NYSE's competitive position, but to protect customer interests by assuring a greater opportunity for interaction of orders without a dealer involved. The SEC has repealed Rule 390 on the premise that whatever benefit Rule 390 may have provided no longer justifies its anticompetitive nature. Rule 390 applied to 30% of the NYSE's listings, accounting for approximately 50% of the exchange's volume in 1999. Much of the anti-390 sentiment was generated by ECN stakeholders, such as Goldman, Merrill, J.P. Morgan, and other large investment banks. Off-board trading restrictions such as Rule 390 have long been questioned as attempts by exchanges with dominant market shares to prohibit competition from other market centers. The elimination of Rule 390, besides boosting the activity of ECNs, also enables broker-dealers to keep more order flow in-house. These restrictions run contrary to the Security Exchange Act of 1934's objectives of assuring fair competition among market centers and eliminating unnecessary burdens on the competition.[2] The NYSE has defended Rule 390 on the basis that it was intended to address market fragmentation by promoting interaction of investor orders without the participation of a dealer; however, the rule also restricts competitive opportunities of ECNs, which use innovative technology that also offers investors a high degree of order interaction. In 2000, the NYSE launched NYSE Direct, an automated service system, which currently executes 10% of the exchange's volume. By 2004, 20% of the volume for stocks listed on the NYSE was executed by NASDAQ or via another ECN. In April 2005, the NYSE decided to merge with Chicago-based Archipelago Holdings Inc, the third largest electronic market for U.S. equities. The objective of the merger is to capitalize on the NYSE's hybrid model. According to the NYSE's Web site, the NYSE Hybrid Market is an innovative response to customer's needs, which integrates into one platform the best aspects of both the auction market and automatic trading. Under the deal with Archipelago, which accounts for nearly 25% of NASDAQ's trading volume, the NYSE is expected to enter

---

[2] "NYSE Rulemaking: Notice of Extension of Comment Period for Issues Relating to Market Fragmentation," Release No. 34-42723 (File No. SR-NYSE-99-48), May 2000, http://www. sec.gov/rules/sro/ny9948n2.htm.

into derivatives and OTC trading is expected to become more competitive with NASDAQ.

4.4 Exchanges Scramble to Consolidate

The recent merger activity with stock exchanges has been a result of new technologies automating trade process flow such as ECNs, and regulatory intervention such as the repeal of Rule 390. This could lead to huge cost savings such as integrating two platforms, or abandoning one of the inferior electronic trading platform. Other advantages of merging include a freeze or reduction in head count for merged entities, thus cutting redundant jobs and reducing the need for office rental, marketing functions, and other systems maintenance. According to Wharton professor Richard J. Herring, "There's an obvious advantage in centralizing exchanges; bigger exchanges enjoy economies of scale that reduces trading costs." The improved liquidity helps share prices to respond more quickly and accurately to changes in supply and demand. Professor Franklin Allen at Wharton states, "There is a drive to have a single market in financial services. At the moment, Europe has too many exchanges. Clearing and settlement aren't nearly as smooth as they should be, and transaction costs are too high." Laws such as Sarbanes-Oxley make it difficult for U.S. exchanges to compete with foreign exchanges in Europe due to regulation being less stringent outside the United States. A merger between a U.S. exchange with another European entity may provide a solution.[3]

4.5 Arguments Against Exchanges

The advancement of technology has enhanced all forms of communication, allowing markets to operate worldwide. The majority is operated by hedge funds, mutual funds, pension funds, and insurance companies. Institutional shareholders are becoming increasingly sophisticated and cost conscious. They worry about potentially questionable practices sometimes found at traditional auction-type exchanges. For example, a floor specialist who knows what his big institutional customer is willing to pay for a block of stock can sometimes buy the stock himself at a lower price, and then sell it to the customer at a higher price. This activity is known as "front running." In order to promote the best prices and to squeeze costs, institutional

---

[3] Marshall E. Blume, "LSE, NYSE, OMX, NASDAQ, Euronext...Why Stock Exchanges Are Scrambling to Consolidate," *Knowledge@Wharton*, March 2006.

investors have pressed for greater computerization and a move away from human intervention found on traditional trading floors.[4]

Monopoly

In a monopoly, the necessary competitive pressures are absent. A monopolist will potentially provide an inferior product, and provide shoddy rules of corporate governance and disclosure. A rational monopolist is expected to offer the same corporate governance and disclosure rules as a competitive exchange but offer the services at a higher price. The repeal of Rule 390 has led the way for electronic communication networks (ECN). The exchanges have traditionally operated as a nonprofit entity owned by its member brokers. The increasing pressure from ECNs has shifted the exchanges toward demutualization and for-profit status. A nonprofit status allows the exchanges to enforce inefficient rules and desired distribution of revenue, but not necessarily maximizing investor welfare. Once an exchange faces substantial competition, it can no longer afford the luxury of designing rules to create the desired distribution among its members.[5]

Competition

The move to a for-profit status will increase an exchange's incentives to adopt optimal investor protections precisely because such protections lead to greater profits. When exchanges are the principal source of disclosure rules in a nonprofit environment, the exchanges have less of an incentive to vigorously investigate alleged violations for a listed company, because of fear that the company will leave to be listed on a competing exchange. The incumbent exchange will most likely back down, unwilling to risk losing a listed company. Competition between exchanges for listings will lead to better regulatory enforcement.[6]

Externalities

The exchange does not sell its services or have the incentive to disclose its corporate governance rules to third parties that happen to trade in a

---

[4] Marshall E. Blume, "LSE, NYSE, OMX, NASDAQ, Euronext . . . Why Stock Exchanges Are Scrambling to Consolidate," *Knowledge@Wharton*, March 2006.
[5] Paul G. Mahoney, "Public and Private Rule Making in Securities Markets," Cato Institute Policy Analysis No. 498, November 2003: 6.
[6] Paul G. Mahoney, "Public and Private Rule Making in Securities Markets," Cato Institute Policy Analysis No. 498, November 2003: 7–8.

particular stock. As a result, the exchange will put less effort into designing and enforcing the rules.[7]

POOR ENFORCEMENT TOOLS

The exchange has little incentive to take action against a listed company that violates its regulations. Should a listed company violate the exchange rules, and the exchange suspends trading in the listed company's stock, it would harm investors and exchange members as much or more than the listed firm. The primary threat the exchange has against a listed company is delisting. In most instances, delisting is an excessive sanction for minor violations and often not credible.[8]

4.6 The Exchanges in the News

The NYSE has been able to maintain monopolistic control of companies listed on its exchange up to 2001, when Rule 390, a regulation that prevented companies listed on the NYSE before 1979 to engage in off-floor transactions, was repealed. After this rule was lifted, stocks listed on the exchange were freely tradable in the over-the-counter (OTC) markets. In 2000, the NYSE launched NYSE Direct+, an automated service system, which currently executes 10% of all trading volume. Technological upgrades have been able to increase trade transparency, but did not necessarily address the underlying problems faced by the exchange such as its mutual ownership structure. The NYSE's 1,366 member-owners, also known as seat holders, have been under financial pressure. The pressure to integrate its electronic platform has moved the NYSE to merge with Chicago-based Archipelago Holdings Inc, the third-largest electronic market for U.S. equities. On April 20, 2005, John Thain, the CEO of the NYSE, announced the merger with Archipelago's CEO Jerry Putnam. The new public, for-profit institution was called the NYSE Group Inc. The merger was designed to promote NYSE current hybrid market, which integrates into one platform the best aspects of both an auction market and automated trading, according to the NYSE. NYSE Arca operates the first open, all-electronic stock exchange in the United States and has a leading position in trading exchange-traded funds and exchange-listed securities. NYSE Arca is also an exchange for trading

---

[7] Paul G. Mahoney, "Public and Private Rule Making in Securities Markets," Cato Institute Policy Analysis No. 498, November 2003: 9.

[8] Ibid.: 11.

equity options. NYSE Arca's trading platform links traders to multiple U.S. market centers and provides customers with fast, electronic, open, direct, and anonymous market access.[9]

NYSE AND ARCAEX

The NYSE and Archipelago merger allows the NYSE to compete more effectively in the post-Regulation NMS market, but in order to facilitate this, it needed a stronger technology foundation with experienced technology staff and entrepreneurial management. The Securities and Exchange Commission adopted the National Market System (NMS), which was implemented to serve two main functions. It was designed to facilitate trading of OTC stocks whose size, profitability, and trading activity meet specific criteria, and it was designed to post prices for securities on the NYSE and other regional exchanges simultaneously, allowing investors to obtain the best prices. The addition of Archipelago provides the NYSE with entry into the listed options business. The merger provides the NYSE with good front-end technology since Archipelago has good aggregation and direct market access technology. This allows order flow to be better managed, controlling flexible order types, routing orders to multiple trading venues, and taking advantage of trading opportunities.

THE NYSE GROUP INC AND EURONEXT N.V. MERGER

On June 1, 2006, the NYSE Group and Euronext N.V. announced a merger of equals combining the leading U.S. and pan-European securities exchanges. According to the NYSE, the combined entity known as NYSE Euronext will be the world's most liquid marketplace, with average daily trading volume of approximately 80 billion euros with total market capitalization of the listed companies of $27 trillion. Both parties believe the merger will create substantial value for all stakeholders through pre-tax annual cost and revenue synergies estimated at 295 million euros. Approximately 195 million euros will result from the overall rationalization of the combined group's IT systems and platforms. NYSE Euronext's three cash trading systems and three derivatives trading systems will be migrated to a single global cash and a single global derivatives platform.[10] NYSE Euronext creates a truly global marketplace solidifying its position as the world's leading listings platform.

---

[9] The NYSE Group Inc., "NYSE Group and EURONEXT N.V. Agree to a Merger of Equals," news release, http://www.nyse.com/press/1149157439121.html.
[10] Ibid.

About Euronext N.V.

Euronext N.V. is the first genuinely cross-border exchange organization in Europe. It provides services for regulated stock and derivatives markets in Belgium, France, the Netherlands, and Portugal, as well as in the U.K. (derivatives only). It is Europe's leading stock exchange based on trading volumes on the central order book. Euronext is integrating its markets across Europe to provide users with a single market that is very broad, highly liquid, and extremely cost-effective. In 2004, it completed a four-year project in which it migrated its markets to harmonized IT platforms for cash trading (NSC), derivatives (LIFFE CONNECT), and clearing. Euronet's development and integration model generates synergies by incorporating the individual strengths and assets of each local market, proving that the most successful way to merge European exchanges is to apply global vision at a local level.[11]

The NASDAQ Stock Market, Inc Purchases Instinet Group

On April 22, 2005, the NASDAQ Stock Market announced a definitive agreement to purchase Instinet Group Incorporated and to sell Instinet's Institutional Broker division to Silver Lake Partners. As a result NASDAQ will own INET ECN. NASDAQ is the largest electronic screen–based equities securities market in the United States. With approximately 3,250 companies, it lists more companies and, on average, trades more shares per day than any other U.S. market. The combined entities will provide investors with a technologically superior trading platform to help NASDAQ operate more competitively in a post-Regulation NMS environment. According to Bob Greifeld, president and CEO of NASDAQ, "Regulation NMS has defined the new competitive landscape by calling for all market centers to be mutually accessible. With this move, we maintain our status as the low-cost provider and at the same time provide increased order interaction for both NASDAQ and exchange-listed securities. We also believe this further enhances our ability to attract new listings." The acquisition is expected to realize significant cost savings with the help of INET technology, and reduce clearing costs as well as corporate expenses through the combined entity. INET, the electronic marketplace, trades about 25% of the NASDAQ listed volume daily and is one of the largest liquidity pools in NASDAQ-listed securities.[12]

---

[11] The NYSE Group Inc., "NYSE Group and EURONEXT N.V. Agree to a Merger of Equals," news release, http://www.nyse.com/press/1149157439121.html.

[12] "NASDAQ to Acquire Instinet," press release, April 22, 2005, http://www.nasdaq.com/newsroom/news/pr2005/ne_section05_044.stm.

THE CHICAGO MERCANTILE EXCHANGE ACQUIRES CHICAGO BOARD OF TRADE

The Chicago Mercantile Exchange has agreed to acquire smaller rival Chicago Board of Trade. The combined entities would be the world's largest derivatives market by trading volume, according to the CME.

4.7 Conclusion

Regulatory intervention such as the repeal of Rule 390 and the introduction of Reg NMS will undoubtedly offer more competition such as better bid and offer spreads, but it has also forced exchanges to speed up and develop new technology. This will allow floor brokers and specialists to interact better with electronic order flow. This new structure has forced exchanges to be flexible, more reactive to customer needs through offering enhanced direct market access technology. This option will allow customers to route order via multiple venues, and take better advantage of trading opportunity.

Chapter 5

Algorithmic Strategies

5.1 Introduction

A significant factor for the growth of algorithms has been the reduction of soft dollar commissions the sell side charges to maintain a relationship with investment managers. Research departments on the sell side are funded through trading commissions generated by the respective trading desk. The buy side will typically award a percentage of their business to a particular sell-side firm in exchange for access to research and maintaining a relationship. The reduction of soft dollar commissions charged by broker-dealers will further promote algorithmic penetration and make them more sophisticated. This is achieved through executing trades via the most efficient and competitively priced venue, rather than doing business with a particular trading desk at a less efficient price in exchange for research subsidized by the soft dollars paid for by the buy side. The efficiency of measuring trades depends on the set of data available. The sell side must time-stamp and report a transaction; however, the buy side is not obligated to do so. The only way to directly compare any two trades is on the basis of both time-stamped data.[1] The most suitable strategy must be evaluated for performance comparisons with the growth and widespread use of algorithmic trading. Having more algorithms at the trader's disposal provides both opportunities and challenges. On the upside, a trader now has the opportunity to pick the suitable algorithm that will most likely achieve the trading objective for each

---

[1] Iain Morse, "European Algo Trading," *Electronic Trading Outlook, Wall Street Letter*, June 2006: 25, http://www.rblt.com/documents/hybridsupplement.pdf.

order. On the down side, the number of algorithm choices can be so large as to make it difficult to make a quick and correct choice.[2]

5.2 Algorithmic Penetration

The utilization of algorithmic trading has advanced as participants strive for better execution prices for their investment objectives. The algorithmic penetration is illustrated in Exhibit 5.1. The buy side is increasingly searching for solutions to lower transaction costs and enhance the quality of their executions, which are being more closely monitored and scrutinized. Algorithmic trading offers a less expensive option to full service brokers, while providing a way to complete a complex order type. Large firms are looking to outsource their trading desks to increase their capacity to execute more volume. Major brokerage houses are franchising their computer trading strategies to smaller firms. Small and midsize broker-dealers who previously lacked resources and time to invest in developing their own Volume-Weighted Average Price (VWAP) strategies can now offer the trading to their buy-side customers. Market fragmentation drives traders to use electronic tools to aid them in accessing the market in different ways.

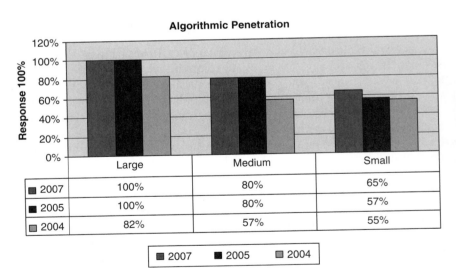

Algorithmic Penetration

	Large	Medium	Small
■ 2007	100%	80%	65%
■ 2005	100%	80%	57%
▨ 2004	82%	57%	55%

■ 2007   ■ 2005   ▨ 2004

Exhibit 5.1   *Source:* TABB Group, June 2005.

---

[2] Jian Yang and Brett Jiu, "Algorithm Selection: A Quantitative Approach," *Algorithmic Trading II: Precision, Control, Execution*, April 2006: 4–8, http://www.itginc.com/news_events/research_papers.php.

Pre-trade analysis has become essential in assessing the suitability of orders that can be appropriately handled by algorithms. If an algorithmic trade is deemed acceptable for a particular order, traders subsequently need to address macro- and micro-level issues. Macro-level decisions include specification of desired benchmark price, and implementation goals. Micro-level decisions include specifying any desired deviation rules. This includes how the algorithm should deviate depending on changing stock prices, market movement, or a change in index or sector values as well as changing market conditions. Micro-level decisions also include specification of order submission rules such as market or limit order, display size, wait periods, order revisions, and modifications or cancellations. Pre-trade analysis provides necessary data to make these informed decisions. It provides investors with liquidity summaries, cost and risk estimates, as well as trading difficulty and stability measures to determine which orders can be successfully implemented via an algorithm or an order that requires manual intervention. It can provide insight into potential risk reduction and hedging opportunities to further improve execution. Pre-trade analysis also provides investors with the necessary data to develop views for short-term price movement and market conditions.

The current trend observed in financial markets is the increasing use of electronic trading tied to a specific benchmark. The benefit of benchmarking is creating measurability. The more common benchmarks can be categorized into pre-, intra-, or post-trade prices. The pre-trade benchmark prices are also known as implementation shortfall. These are known prices recognized before or at the time trading begins. These include previous night's closing price, opening price, and price at the time of order entry. Intraday benchmarks are composed of prices that occur during a trading session, at the average of open, high, low, or close. Pricing schemes such as the Order Submission Rules refer to share quantities, wait periods between order submissions, revisions, and cancellations. The more common pricing rules include market and limit orders as well as floating prices that are pegged to a reference price such as the bid, ask, or midpoint and change with the reference price. These order types allow algorithms to utilize the optimally prescribed strategy by executing aggressively or passively when needed. Post-trade benchmarks include any prices that occur after the end of trading, or the day's closing price. Post-trade analysis consists of cost measurement and algorithm performance analysis. Cost is measured as the difference between the actual realized execution price and the specified benchmark price. This allows investors to critique the accuracy of the trading cost model to improve future cost estimates and provides investment managers with higher-quality price information. Algorithmic performance is assessed through its ability to follow through with the optimally prescribed strategy. Post-trade analysis is important to ensure that broker-dealers are delivering the advertised pre-trade cost estimates.[3]

5.3 Implementation Shortfall Measurement

An optimal trading strategy begins with the accurate measurement of trading costs and implementation shortfall. Andre Perold[4] defines implementation shortfall as the difference in return between a theoretical portfolio and the implemented portfolio. In a paper portfolio, a portfolio manager looks at prevailing prices, in relation to execution prices in an actual portfolio. Implementation shortfall measures the price distance between the final, realized trade price, and a pre-trade decision price. According to Barclays Global Investors,[5] implementation shortfall can be distinguished by three categories: the paper portfolio, the actual portfolio, and the "rabbit portfolio."

1. **Paper portfolio**   The paper portfolio represents the ideal situation. All securities are transacted at benchmark prices. Transaction costs, commissions, bid-ask spread, liquidity impact, opportunity costs, market trends, and slippage do not happen.
2. **Actual portfolio**   The actual portfolio reflects reality; all securities are transacted in real markets. Market impact, commissions, bid-ask spread, liquidity, opportunity costs, and slippage are factored in.
3. **Rabbit portfolio**   The "rabbit" portfolio represents expected trading costs; all securities are transacted in expected markets. The paper portfolio has no trading costs. The actual portfolio has high trading costs. The rabbit portfolio falls somewhere between the two. The rabbit portfolio is the benchmark by which traders measure performance.

A portfolio manager places an order to buy 700 shares of XYZ. This order is filled through the course of three days. The order was issued on Day 0 after the close. On Day 1, the trader purchased 300 shares at $101.00, and the market closed at $102.00 that day. On Day 2, the trader purchased an additional 200 shares at a price of $101.75; the market closed at $102.50 on Day 2. On Day 3, the trader purchased another 100 shares at a price of $102.50 with a market close of $102.75. Only 600 shares were executed with

---

[3] Robert Kissell, Roberto Malamut, PhD, "Understanding the Profit and Loss Distribution of Trading Algorithms," Originally published in *Institutional Investor*, Guide to Algorithmic Trading, Spring 2005.

[4] André F. Perold, "The Implementation Shortfall: Paper vs. Reality," *Journal of Portfolio Management* 14, no. 3 (Spring 1988).

[5] Minder Cheng, "Pretrade Cost Analysis and Management of Implementation Shortfall," AIMR Conference Proceedings July 2003, no. 7 (DOI 10.2469/cp.v2003.n7.3349).

Table 5.1   Data for 700-Share Order (only 600 shares were executed)

Day	Price of Close	Trade Price	Number of Shares
0	$100.00	$100.00	0
1	$102.00	$101.00	300
2	$102.50	$101.75	200
3	$102.75	$102.50	100

Source: http:// www.aimrpubs.org 2003.

100 shares left behind. The average price of the 600 shares was $101.50 (see Table 5.1).

The implementation shortfall is illustrated in Exhibit 5.2. The top line is the paper portfolio return, which assumes that on Day 1, all 700 shares were traded at the previous night's close of $100 per share. At the end of Day 1, when the stock closed at $102, the paper portfolio showed a $2 per-share profit, for a total profit of $2 × 700, or $1,400. Because all 700 shares were traded on Day 1, on Day 2, the profit was $2.50 per share for all 700 shares, or $1,750 total.

The second line is the actual portfolio return. On Day 1, only 300 shares were bought at $101.00, rather than at the previous day's close of $100. The $291 reflects the $1 per-share profit earned on those 300 shares minus the commission of 3 cents per share. On Day 2, 200 more shares were bought at

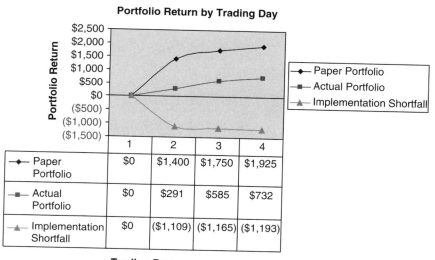

Portfolio Return by Trading Day

	1	2	3	4
Paper Portfolio	$0	$1,400	$1,750	$1,925
Actual Portfolio	$0	$291	$585	$732
Implementation Shortfall	$0	($1,109)	($1,165)	($1,193)

Trading Day

Exhibit 5.2   Implementation shortfall example. *Source:* http://www.aimrpubs.org 2003.

$101.75, with the profit for those shares being $102.50 less the trade price and commission cost, for a total of $144. This amount was added to the appreciation of the 300 shares that were purchased on Day 1. Those 300 shares earned $.50 per share or $150 on Day 2. The total Day 2 profit was $585 (the Day 1 profit on the 300 shares of $291 plus the Day 2 profit on the 200 shares of $144 plus the incremental profit on the 300 Day 1 shares of $150). The Day 3 profit would be calculated similarly.

The implementation shortfall is the difference between the top two lines. On Day 1, the difference between the actual and paper portfolios was $1,109. On the second day, the difference was $1,165, and on the third day it was $1,193. The implementation shortfall on this trade was $1,193.

5.4 Volume-Weighted Average Price

The Volume-Weighted Average Price, commonly known as VWAP, remains the primary benchmark for algorithmic trading. Daily VWAP can be calculated through the record of daily stock transactions. VWAP is defined as the dollar amount traded for every transaction (price times shares traded) divided by the total shares traded for a given day. The method of judging VWAP is simple. If the price of a buy order is lower than the VWAP, the trade is considered good; if the price is higher, it is considered poor. Performance of traders is evaluated through their ability to execute orders at prices better than the volume-weighted average price over a given trade horizon. Volume is an important market characteristic for participants who aim to lower the market impact of their trades. This impact can be measured through comparing the execution price of an order to a benchmark. The VWAP benchmark is the sum of every transaction price paid, weighted by its volume.

VWAP strategies introduce a time dimension in the order execution process. If the trader cannot control whether the trade will be executed during the day, VWAP strategies allow the order to dilute the impact of orders through the day.

Most institutional trading occurs in filling orders that exceed the daily volume. When large numbers of shares must be traded, liquidity concerns can affect price goals. For this reason, some firms offer multiday VWAP strategies to respond to customers' requests. In order to further reduce the market impact of large orders, customers can specify their own volume participation by limiting the volume of their orders on low expected volume days. Each order is sliced into several days' orders and then sent to a VWAP engine for the corresponding days.

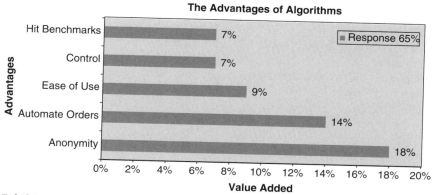

Exhibit 5.3 Survey of buy-side traders.

Some trades and trading prices reflect objectives that cannot be captured by a VWAP analysis. For example, value managers are looking for underpriced situations. They buy stock and wait to sell it until good news raises its prices (see Exhibit 5.3). Growth managers react to good news, which hopefully leads to more good news. While growth managers buy on good news, value managers sell. Consequently growth managers have a clear trading disadvantage (see Exhibit 5.4) because they buy when the buying interest dominates the market. Automated algorithms cannot take this into account in trading.[6]

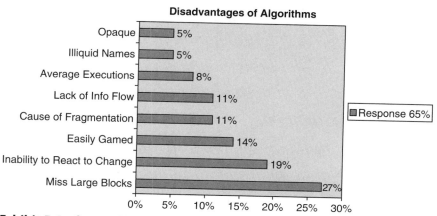

Exhibit 5.4 *Source:* TABB Group, June 2005.

[6] Jedrzeij Bialkowski, Serge Darolles, and Gaëlle LeFol, "Decomposing Volume for VWAP Strategies" (Working Papers no. 2005-16, Centre de Recherche en Economique et Statistique), http://www.crest.fr/doctravail/document/2005-16.pdf.

5.5 VWAP Definitions

VWAP strategies (see Table 5.2) are utilized to maximize best execution and ensure the lowest trading cost. Trading costs are usually computed by comparing the average realized transaction price against a reference or benchmark price. The choice of a performance benchmark will affect a trader's decisions regarding order placement strategies such as limit vs. market orders, trading horizons, and venues such as primary markets, upstairs markets, and crossing systems. These decisions have significant impact on realized trading costs. Daily VWAP benchmarks encourage traders to spread their trades over time to avoid the risk of trading at prices

Table 5.2   Different VWAP Strategies

Measure	Definition	Remarks
Full VWAP	Ratio of the dollar volume traded to the corresponding share volume over the trading horizon, including all transactions	Standard definition, usually computed the day of the trade. Multiday VWAP are orders broken up for execution over several days, or intraday VWAP for orders executed strictly within the trading day.
VWAP excluding own transactions	Ratio of dollar volume traded (excluding own volume) to share volume over the trading horizon	When a trader's order is a large fraction of volume, excluding the trader's own transaction volume, this may produce a misrepresentative benchmark.
Non-block VWAP	VWAP computed excluding upstairs or block trades	Excluding large block trades is reasonable for small traders who cannot access upstairs liquidity. While some markets flag upstairs trades, others including those in the United States do not. It is common t exclude trades of 10,000 or more shares as a proxy for upstairs trades.
VWAP proxies	Proxies for VWAP, including simple average of open, low, high, and close	In emerging markets where tick-level data are unavailable, proxies are readily computed.
Value-weighted average price	Prices weighted by dollar value of trade, not share volume	Value-weighting is reasonable for volatile securities because the weights are determined by the economic value of the transaction. Other weight schemes also exist.

Source: Ananth Madhavan, VWAP Strategies.

that are at the extreme for the day. This practice entails significant risks, because delay and opportunity costs arising from passive participation trading can erode significantly.

VWAP strategies fall into three categories: Sell order to a broker-dealer who guarantees VWAP; cross the order at a future date at VWAP; or trade the order with the goal of achieving a price of VWAP or better (see Table 5.3).

Guaranteed principal VWAP bid offers an execution to be guaranteed at VWAP for a fixed per-share commission, and the broker-dealer assumes the entire risk of failing to meet the benchmark. The predetermined cost in commissions is often attractive, but the true cost of the guaranteed VWAP bid could be very high. The broker-dealer is taking on the risk of the trade, hoping to profit by executing the trade at prices that beat the VWAP. This can occur through a variety of ways. The client's trade list may include names of securities in which the broker-dealer seeks to take the same position, or the broker-dealer can benefit from knowledge of the client's flows prior to the client executing the order through the broker.

A forward VWAP cross pre-commits the trader to execute at a price that is not known in advance. Crossing allows both buyers and sellers to avoid price impact, which is usually significantly higher than the commission cost. However, both sides face price risks in the event of a significant market movement.

Table 5.3 VWAP Strategies

Strategy	Providers	Advantages	Disadvantages
Guaranteed principal VWAP bid	Major broker-dealers	Low commission, guaranteed execution	Exposure to significant adverse price movements; leakage of information in thinly traded stocks
Forward VWAP cross	Ashton Technology Group, Instinet	Low commission, no market impact	Non-execution risk; residual must be traded. Exposure to significant adverse price movements
Agency trading or direct market access	Major broker-dealers	Control over trading process, including ability to cancel during the day	VWAP is not guaranteed. Commission costs; ticket charges add up. Significant time commitment
Automated participation strategy	ITG SmartServer, FlexTrade, Madoff	Ability to cancel during the day; low cost and can be somewhat customized	VWAP is not guaranteed. Possibility shortfalls on days with unusual price or volume patterns

Source: Ananth Madhavan, VWAP Strategies.

In VWAP trading, clients may trade orders themselves via direct market access, or give them to a broker-dealer. This gives clients price protection through limit prices (the ability to stop or cancel trading, or the ability to control where the order is traded or how). Typically, the order is broken up for execution over the day to participate in the day's volume. Control of transaction costs is the key to minimizing the shortfall from VWAP. Traders may also try to use their expertise and their specific knowledge to beat the VWAP.

5.6 Time-Weighted Average Price

TWAP stands for Time-Weighted Average Price and allows traders to "time-slice" a trade over a certain period of time. Unlike VWAP, which typically trades less stock when market volume dips, TWAP will trade the same amount of stock spread out throughout the time period specified in the order. This is an attractive alternative to trading orders, which are not dependent on volume. This scenario can overcome obstacles such as fulfilling orders in illiquid stocks with unpredictable volume.

EXAMPLE OF A TWAP ORDER

At 2:00 pm in the afternoon, a trader wishes to exit a position in an illiquid stock by the 4:00 pm close but does not wish to execute more than 25% of total volume in that stock during that given time frame.

- Trader puts in sell order for 50,000 shares of XYZ.
- Volume constraint is set at 25%.
- A limit price is set as a price protection.
- A start time of 2:00 pm and an end time of 4:00 pm is specified as a time interval.

MARKET SHARE

The complexity of an algorithm may be measured by the number of different strategies implemented. Each strategy has its own pros and cons. As firms become more sophisticated about algorithms, their demands for more flexible customized products will increase (see Exhibit 5.5). Simple VWAP models have a disadvantage because this strategy can discourage block trading, which leads to market fragmentation or striving for average. It discourages traders from making large bets.

Algorithms have a lower cost structure than a human-based trading floor. Brokers are able to charge low commissions for algorithms as computing costs continue to fall. Many firms believe that low- or no-touch offerings are essential to their business. Competition in this market will become fiercer as

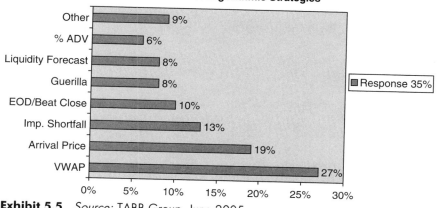

Exhibit 5.5 *Source:* TABB Group, June 2005.

more firms enter the market. Amid the ever intensifying battle for algorithmic supremacy, one in which there are plenty of potent and proven programs from which to choose; Credit Suisse's Advanced Execution Services (AES) is one of the most frequently cited as being somewhere ahead of the pack. Credit Suisse was most often mentioned as the algorithmic provider of choice.[7] The broker algorithm market share has been dominated by those

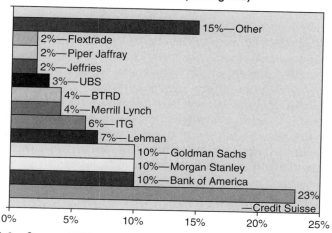

Exhibit 5.6 *Source:* TABB Group, June 2005.

[7] "Algo Arms Race has a leader—for now", Securities Industry News, www.securitiesindustry. com, December 18, 2006.

Algorithm Leaders Weighted by AUM

Other	10%
Nomura	5%
UNX	3%
Citigroup	5%
BNY	5%
ITG	5%
Piper Jaffray	5%
Morgan Stanley	7%
Merrill Lynch	8%
Bank of America	9%
Lehman	10%
Goldman	11%
Credit Suisse	18%

Exhibit 5.7   *Source:* TABB Group, June 2005.

with the quickest reaction time to market (see Exhibits 5.6 and 5.7). Buy-side firms are now looking for how broker-dealers can package additional products into electronic trading. As of now, other market segments such as fixed-income instruments have hardly been tapped. The brokerage firms with the keenest vision, the best tools, and the most comprehensive support will have a clear advantage.

5.7 Conclusion

Volume-Weighted Average Price (VWAP), Time-Weighted Average Price (TWAP), implementation shortfall, and arrival price represent the basic algorithms a brokerage firm will provide. Some brokers have made substantial investments in sophisticated algorithms, while for other brokers, algorithms are simply another method of generating business despite being a loss leader simply to help the firm's bottom line. Bulge-bracket firms are most likely to develop their algorithms in-house, investing significant amounts in constantly refining their offerings. They will also use statistics and trade data based on internal algorithmic flows to determine transaction costs and market impact costs. Smaller niche brokers may go with vendor solutions that charge a flat fee. Agency brokers feel they have an advantage in providing nonproprietary services that service the customer alone. A bulge-bracket firm may utilize client flow analyzing the data for their own proprietary trading desk. The large broker-dealers still dominate the algorithm market, but agency brokers are gaining momentum due to their neutral stance.[8]

---

[8] Daniel Safarik, "Algorithmic Trading: Somehow, It All Adds Up," *Wall Street & Technology*, August 7, 2006.

Chapter 6

Algorithmic Feasibility and Limitations

6.1 Introduction

Algorithms are most effective and feasible for trades too small to focus on, or too liquid for a human trader to add impact or add significant value. One way to measure the performance of an algorithm is through transaction cost analysis (TCA). It presents a way for buy-side traders to scrutinize the quality of their executions. Equity markets are easily analyzed given regulatory boards and exchanges report historical transactions. Markets such as foreign exchange however have a fairly arbitrary process for measuring algorithmic performance. There is no aggregated volume information available for foreign exchange because the traditional approach has been the Request for Quote (RFQ) model instead of trading through an exchange with little or no regulatory insight, making an exact volume weighted average price (VWAP) calculation difficult. Some foreign exchange ECNs such as Currenex and the prime brokerage division of an investment bank may provide traders the ability to calculate performance based on historical benchmarks, which have been calculated hourly based on published algorithms.

Some of the limitations of using algorithms include unrealistic expectations of what algorithms can do. Algorithms are not the optimal trading strategy for every order. Utilizing pre-trade tools combined with analyzing post-trade order flow and performance analysis provides a statistical method for determining the optimal trading approach.

6.2 Trade Structure

Constructing algorithms involves a sequence of structured or unstructured trades seeking liquidity, generally linked to a certain benchmark such as VWAP. A structured approach involves tracking strategies based on historical data, or strategy benchmarks, while unstructured liquidity is generally associated with real-time information or price benchmarks. Certain pre-trade information is required to determine which structure to implement:

1. **Trade horizon** Short horizons require less structure. A half-hour VWAP trade and a similarly timed pegging and discretion strategy will not yield a significantly different outcome.
2. **Need to finish** The higher the need to finish an order, the more structure is needed, in order to avoid falling behind schedule. The type of pre-trade information here relates more to portfolio manager instructions than to specific analytics.
3. **Predictability** The degree of predictability governs the degree to which horizon and schedule should be implemented. This consideration requires the use of properties of the distribution estimates, in addition to averages, such as standard deviation measures.
4. **Price sensitivity** As price sensitivity increases, structure becomes less useful, due to the need to advertise willingness to trade. Short-term volatility history and real-time deviation are inputs along the dimension.
5. **Risk tolerance** Refers to execution risks versus the benchmark. Greater tolerance generates less need for a structured horizon and schedule. Pre-trade information can map out optimal tradeoffs between risk, cost, and alpha for varying trade horizons.[1]

6.3 Algorithmic Feasibility

Not all trade orders are suitable for an algorithmic strategy. Two questions must be answered before any further consideration for analysis can be performed. First, is the order suitable for algorithmic trading? And if so, which algorithm is the optimal one for the trading order? Once the suitability for an algorithm and an appropriate benchmark are determined the next step is to decide which algorithm among the many available should be used to trade an order. One such strategy can be VWAP. The appeal for utilizing VWAP as a strategy is its ease of attainability. A trader can slice orders

---

[1] Ian Domowitz and Henry Yegerman, "Measuring and Interpreting the Performance of Broker Algorithms," in *Algorithmic Trading: A Buy-Side Handbook*, 67–70 (London: The Trade Ltd., 2005).

within a certain time interval. Even if there are significant stock price moves during the day, either due to market impacts of the trading or due to the stock's volatility, VWAP can be attained over a given time horizon. However, one of the limitations of utilizing VWAP is the fact that it pays no attention to the size of the trade especially if the filling order exceeds one day's volume. There is no reference to address what such a trade should cost. The cost of trading in size is valuable to traders and portfolio managers who must decide if such a large order is worthy enough to cover the expected in-and-out trading costs.

There are numerous arguments for utilizing algorithms:[2]

1. **Increased capacity** Algorithms handle the manual and computationally intensive processes, freeing up traders to focus on more complex issues as well as to handle more flow efficiently.
2. **Decreased costs** Commissions for electronic trading tend to be significantly lower than for phone trades worked manually.
3. **Real-time feedback and control** Algorithmic trading should not be considered a "set it and forget it" proposition. To get the most out of algorithms, the trader should monitor executions and impact in real time, modifying execution parameters or trading strategies to adapt to changing market conditions, executions not working as expected, and movements in correlated assets.
4. **Anonymity** With algorithmic trading, no one ever knows who is sending the orders; sometimes they don't even know that the order has been sent at all. Orders can be worked across multiple brokers.
5. **Control of information leakage** In addition to the anonymity-related benefits described above, algorithmic trading precludes traders from having to expose their alpha expectations to anyone outside the office.
6. **Access to multiple trading venues** Algorithms can make instantaneous decisions where to route orders. This not only applies to multilisted securities, but also allows orders to be exposed to crossing networks and internal flow.
7. **Consistent execution methodology** Consistent execution was the driving force behind the creation of benchmarks like VWAP. Knowledge of the underlying principles of an algorithm allows a trader to understand why it reacted to a market anomaly as it did.
8. **Best execution and TCA** Real-time TCA, including execution, impact, slippage, and correlation information, is now valuable to both the trader and the portfolio manager versus multiple benchmarks. Because electronic trading time-stamps each movement of

---

[2] Eric Goldberg, "Beyond Market Impact," *The Trade* no. 3, January–March 2005, http://www.tiny.cc/r1UfK.

an order and keeps that information accessible, all types of pre- and post-trade analytics can now be performed and compared.

9. **Minimize errors**   Straight-through processing allows orders to be loaded and executed totally hands-off.

10. **Compliance monitoring**   Compliance rules including limits, exposure, and short sales can be validated in real time, and alerts can be issued for any potential scenario.

6.4 Algorithmic Trading Checklist

The following checklist[3] gives steps that should be followed in order to determine the feasibility for utilizing an algorithm for a particular order:

1. **Nature of algorithmic strategy**   A thorough analysis should be done on the nature of each algorithm before the algorithm is ever used.

2. **Suitability of algorithmic trading**   Some orders are less suitable for execution via an algorithm and may be better handled by humans. These are typically large orders, orders for stocks with difficult liquidity conditions, or those with very specific requirements.

3. **Fit between order and algorithms**   Even if an order is a "normal" one and can be algorithmically traded, the trader must determine which available algorithms are suitable for this particular order. Some algorithms are better under certain circumstances, while others prevail under other conditions. When an algorithmic trading product is offered, the trader must question the vendor regarding "optimal" operating conditions of the product. Some questions include: What are the tradable order sizes? Does the algorithm handle extraordinary low or high volatilities? Is the algorithm time-of-day-dependent?

4. **Choice of benchmark**   Traders often have less flexibility in selecting the benchmark as benchmarks are usually part of the desk's trading policy. How benchmarks are derived and calculated inside the algorithm should also be researched.

6.5 High Opportunity Costs

Traders care most about average costs vs. arrival price along with consistency in cost. The arrival price is defined as the price of a stock at the time the order is raised and used as a pre-trade benchmark to measure

---

[3] Jian Yang and Brett Jiu, "Algorithm Selection: A Quantitative Approach," *Algorithmic Trading II: Precision, Control, Execution*, April 2006: 4–8.

execution quality. The difference between the order arrival price and the execution price can be used to determine the implementation shortfall. The previous day's close price is used as the benchmark when orders are submitted prior to the market opening. A passive algorithm such as VWAP may ensure a good average price vs. arrival price, but it may have shortcomings. VWAP may do a poor job compared to implementation shortfall algorithms in terms of consistency of performance vs. arrival price as the trade size/volume goes down. This is illustrated when the standard deviation of the P&L vs. arrival price of trades against the percent of volume for VWAP and implementation shortfall algorithms is displayed. For example, if stock XYZ trades 50 million shares on an average day, and the trader has 5 million shares to trade, a VWAP algorithm may be appropriate. However, if the trader only has a block of 10,000 shares to execute, then the savings of market impact by slicing the order through the course of a day is not as significant as opposed to the opportunity cost the trader could save by trading the stock and executing the whole order immediately.

VWAP algorithms can potentially suffer from high opportunity costs especially for orders representing a low percentage of ADV. Opportunity cost can be defined as the standard deviation of the trading cost. This is a function of trade distribution, stock volatility, and correlation among stocks on a trade list over a given time frame. Traders can determine trading costs for a given strategy. One method of minimizing the cost is by implementing a participation algorithm, which consists of a constant percentage of the daily volume. A participation algorithm is similar to utilizing VWAP except that a trader can set the volume to a constant percentage of total volume of a given order. For example, a 10% participation algorithm for stock XYZ, which trades 30 million shares of average daily volume, would trade 3 million shares. If the trader wishes to implement an order with market impact caused by 10% participation for stock XYZ, then the trader may use a 10% participation algorithm.

A volume participation algorithm can represent a method of minimizing supply and demand imbalances, but other factors such as order type placement can have an impact as well. For example, spreads and temporary price impact may potentially be higher as the market opens because there is more uncertainty about the future price of a given security through the course of the day. Market makers and liquidity providers tend to be more careful at the beginning of the day and can charge more or try to get a risk premium. An implementation shortfall algorithm should model these factors. Algorithms such as the more popular VWAP and volume participation to more sophisticated ones may reduce implementation shortfalls, but the ideal implementation shortfall algorithm should model the optimal trade by looking at liquidity profile, trade sizes, volatility of stocks, volatility distributions of stocks, spread distributions of stocks, and stock correlations. Algorithmic trading products such as ITG SmartServer and ITG Horizon-Plus can provide implementation shortfall algorithms that model these factors providing the least opportunity cost. These algorithms adjust themselves by looking at real-time conditions and making the best use of historical and real-time data.

6.6 Newsflow Algorithms

Algorithms are evolving from the traditional VWAP benchmark and reading post-trade data to adopting newsflow algorithms.[4] Basic newsflow is already incorporated into some algorithmic trading engines. Kirsti Suutari, the head of global business algorithmic trading for Reuters, believes that newsflow will have particular value when it comes to order-generating strategies. The source of the newsflow from a vendor such as Reuters could format the newsflow or flag specific elements within a news story that would allow an algorithmic trading engine to read the data in the same way as it monitors market data. Flags can be attached by highlighting important elements of a news story such as unexpected financial losses at a company. The shortcomings when it comes to news processing come down to the accuracy of the news itself or the news-analyzing system; others dismiss this as an unrealistic attempt at developing artificial intelligence. Data providers such as Dow Jones and Reuters have several options in developing newsflow services for algorithms, including the following:

- **News flagging** Specialists could flag news to highlight relevant information for clients, according to client-specified benchmarks,
- **News formatting** Scheduled news, such as financial results or corporate actions, could be formatted for easy recognition. Using an agreed-upon standard, the news vendor can format news for a client's system to interpret without the need for specialized catch-all analytical software,
- **Raw news** For firms that prefer to perform the analysis internally, the news source could provide raw news without any formatting or flagging changes. This would leave the burden of news interpretation in the hands of the client—but would remove any doubts about the news vendor influencing the interpretation of a news story,

---

[4] Philip Craig, "Special Report Algorithmic Trading: More News Is Good News," *Waters*, March 1, 2006, http://www.watersonline.com/public/showPage.html?page=318489.

- **News archive**   Reuters has revealed that it is looking at developing an archive of its information, including news stories. In developing an archive of news, vendors could demonstrate correlations between news stories and price movements in much the same way that investment firms use historical market data to test and develop trading strategies based on newsflow.

Whether or not newsflow algorithms will be successfully implemented remains to be seen. "The most effective and complex algorithm is the human," according to Kevin Bourne, global head of execution trading at HSBC. News-reading technologies should have reached the market by the end of 2006.

6.7 Black Box Trading for Fixed-Income Instruments

The feasibility of utilizing an algorithm for fixed-income instruments seems theoretical for the time being. Most electronic trades are executed via a request for quote (RFQ) venue where customers or other dealers retain the ability to refuse a trade request. Fixed-income instruments are also primarily a dealer market. Most algorithms rely on a constant stream of market data, which is not currently available for fixed income markets. Few transactions are posted through a black box because there are few bond trading platforms that provide the necessary liquidity. Currently, the U.S. Treasury market is dominated by eSpeed and Icap where opportunistic traders attempt to arbitrage their positions through purchasing an instrument on one platform and selling it via another. Other electronic venues include TradeWeb and MarketAxess. Electronic trading is made up of two separate markets: interdealer markets where common bonds are quoted anonymously and available for instant execution, and the dealer-to-customer market where trading is not anonymous and customers can see the dealer who is providing quotes. Black box trading has improved transparency and reduced inefficiencies in the Treasuries market, but corporate bonds remain a challenge given that trades are far less frequent and current price information is unavailable. The NASD is making attempts to improve transparency in corporate instruments with TRACE reporting. However, despite regulatory intervention, corporate bond trades are reported within a 15-minute time span and not real time.[5]

---

[5] Daniel Safarik, "Fixed Income Meets the Black Box," *Wall Street & Technology*, October 24, 2005.

In July 2006, the CBOT introduced a pilot program for algorithms utilized for two- and five-year Treasury futures. The pilot program was implemented to assess the impact on trading profiles and behavior; to identify the demographics of participants pre- and post-pilot implementation; to determine whether the change in algorithm impacts the number of participants in a contract; and to assess the growth rate of the five-year Treasury Note contracts benchmarked against relevant instruments along the yield curve. The program was designed to monitor a straight First In First Out (FIFO) algorithm, which matches trades on a strict time and price priority, versus a pro rata algorithm, which matches trades based on a distributed proportionate approach. The exchange will continue to change in contract volume, participation levels, and order management behavior.[6]

6.8 Conclusion

Algorithms are designed to balance a juggling act. They are intended to lower transaction costs, reduce market impact, and create liquidity. A large trade executed through an algorithm should be efficient, creating liquidity and avoiding risk in the event the market moves against you. On the flip side, executing multiple small orders will have little or no market impact, but can take so long to complete the process that it will wind up increasing the chances of factors outside a trader's control moving the market against you. Accessing the right liquidity pools connecting to multiple venues is important. A large order using a number of different algorithms to access the market simultaneously can result in algorithms that conflict with one another. The better algorithms are both predicting and measuring market impact, so strategies can be adjusted in real time. When an order is cut into pieces with multiple algorithms trading at the same time, this can cause brokers to end up competing with themselves.[7]

---

[6] "Trade Matching Algorithm Pilot Program for Five Year Treasury Futures: The Reintroduction of FIFO Match Algorithm," Chicago Board of Trade, October 2006, http://www.cbot.com/cbot/docs/77187.pdf.

[7] Will Sterling, "Algorithmic Trading: A Powerful Tool for an Increasingly Complex Trading Environment," *Electronic Trading Outlook, Wall Street Letter*, June 2006, http://www.rblt.com/documents/hybridsupplement.pdf.

Chapter 7

Electronic Trading Networks

7.1 Introduction

Trading processes have changed significantly with increased communication capacities and technology enabling online orders forwarded directly to the markets. This model, also known as direct market access (DMA), allows traders to execute via venues that are not only low in transaction fees but also eliminate the involvement of a more cost-intensive trader on a trading desk. As the usage of DMA increased, alternative execution venues arose to provide the best avenue. This venue, also known as smart order-routing concepts, is specified by the customer based on different parameters such as price, liquidity, costs, and speed. Third-party software providers such as Belzberg, Firefly Capital, or Lava Trading offer DMA in combination with algorithmic trading, smart order routing, or liquidity aggregation. Electronic communication networks (ECNs) connect smart order-routing systems with this kind of market transparency and enables them to perform order routing, exploiting the increased connectivity of electronic trading systems based on the FIX protocol.[1]

7.2 Direct Market Access

Direct market access has become an integral part of trading technology in the United States since the 1997 order-handling rules facilitated the creation

---

[1] Peter Gomber and Markus Gsell, "Catching Up with Technology: The Impact of Regulatory Changes on ECNs/MTFs and the Trading Venue Landscape in Europe," *Competition and Regulation in Network Industries* (forthcoming).

of ECNs. Firms could get a much quicker integrated view of markets through high-speed aggregation (see Table 7.1). Aggregation technologies provide liquidity in marketplaces as well as creating an execution facility that can trade through multiple trading venues. Aggregators have developed smart routing technology, which analyzes an order, polls the market, and locates the most efficient venue to most effectively execute the trade. The benefits of aggregation technologies have materialized as more investors and institutions access ECNs. According to the TABB Group, the most important feature of aggregation is functionality.

DMA offers investors a direct and efficient method of accessing electronic exchanges through Internet trading. DMA gives the individual an autonomous role in deciding on an investment strategy, matching buyers and sellers directly. This trading methodology allows investors to execute orders through specific destinations such as market makers, exchanges, and electronic communication networks. Some trading may continue to rely on personal contacts, which can be enhanced with instant messaging technology or executing trades through trusted counterparties. DMA has been adopted by buy-side traders to aggregate liquidity that is fragmented across U.S. execution venues. DMA tools permit buy-side traders to execute multiple venues directly without intervention from brokers. The real motivation for DMA trading, however, is cheaper commissions. DMA commissions are about one cent a share, while program trades cost roughly two cents and block trades cost four to five cents per share.

An electronic trading system's market structure includes the trade execution details and the amount of price and quote data it releases. Three generic

Table 7.1   Bulge-Bracket Firms

Firm	Service	Representative Technology Component
Credit Suisse	Advanced Execution Services (AES)	Pathfinder, proprietary
Goldman Sachs	Goldman Sachs Algorithmic Trading (GSAT)	REDIPlus, TradeFactory, TheGuide
JP Morgan	Electronic Execution Services	Proprietary
Lehman Brothers	Lehman Model Execution (LMX)	LehmanLive, LINKS, Portfolio WebBench
Morgan Stanley	Benchmark Execution Services	Passport, Navigator, Scorecard, EPA
Merrill Lynch	ML X-ACT	Proprietary

Source: Firms—Aite Group.

market structure types are a continuous limit order book, a single price auction, and a trading system with passive pricing. In an electronic limit order book, traders post bids and offers on a system for other participants to view. A limit order is an order to buy a specified quantity of a security at or below a specified price. The order book displays orders and ranks them by price and then by time (see Exhibit 7.1). A limit order does not typically display the user's identity, the order's entry time, or the period the order is good for. If a bid or offer is in the book and the participant enters an order outside of the market at the same price or better, the limit order book automatically matches the orders and a trade occurs.

In a single-price auction system, participants may submit bids and offers over a period of time, but the system executes all the trades at the same price at the same time. The system calculates the transaction price to maximize the total volume traded when both bids and offers reside in the system. Some electronic trading systems determine trade prices through referring to other markets' pricing and sales activity. These trading systems have no independent price discovery mechanisms and their prices are taken directly from primary markets as passive.[2]

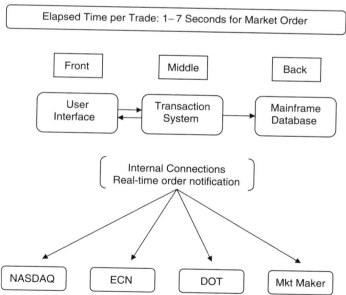

Exhibit 7.1   Direct access brokerage technology model. *Source:* A. B. Watley, Intel and KBW Research.

---

[2] Terrence Hendershott, "Electronic Trading in Financial Markets," *IT Pro*, IEEE Computer Society, July, 2003.

Direct market access has been available on the institutional level through services such as Instinet and REDI. Goldman Sach's REDIPlus, Morgan Stanley's Passport, and Credit Suisse's Pathfinder platforms offer global connectivity to equities, futures, and options exchanges. Niche player NeoNet Securities offers direct access to European equity markets and to U.S. markets for European clients. Interactive Brokers (IB) is adding bond trading to its direct access platform and is using smart routing technology to trade stocks, ETFs, options, futures, and FX. In 2004, Lava Trading launched a direct access product for FX trading.[3] The increase in regulatory pressure will help retail trading and will provide considerable growth within electronic markets. Some participants believe that DMA is a market-data–driven trading platform to access live trading markets; others see it as only a broker link that may include an algorithm. Many DMA providers are currently working on expanding DMA from aggregating liquidity to being a full execution platform. Several DMA platforms have launched multibroker models that allow efficient routing of order flow.

The general benefits of DMA technologies (see Exhibit 7.2) include

- allowing speed of execution and the potential for better pricing for investors that may not have otherwise been provided utilizing a third-party broker/dealer;
- maximizing access to liquidity;

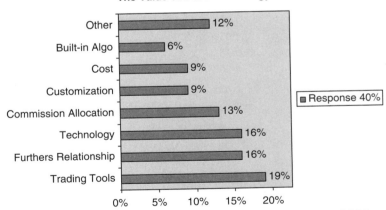

The Value of DMA Technology

Other	12%
Built-in Algo	6%
Cost	9%
Customization	9%
Commission Allocation	13%
Technology	16%
Furthers Relationship	16%
Trading Tools	19%

Response 40%

Exhibit 7.2   *Source: Equity Trading in America*, TABB Group, June 2005.

[3] Daniel Safarik, "Direct Market Access: The Next Frontier," *Wall Street & Technology*, February 28, 2005.

- providing the ability to supply a wide range of order entry functionality allowing for stealthier trading of large blocks;
- access to multiple products and markets.

The current value of DMA technology is changing because the nature of order flow is becoming too difficult to trade without an algorithm. Investors continue to search for an integrated trading platform that brings together market data, access to trading venues, broker and proprietary algorithms, crossing networks and a host of trading tools integrated into order management systems.[4]

7.3 Electronic Communication Networks

One of the major advances in providing better access to markets giving buy-side traders more autonomy has been the ECNs. ECNs offer electronic real-time price discovery, which enables buyers and sellers to transact relatively inexpensively with a minimum of intermediation. The Securities and Exchange Commission (SEC) defines the biggest electronic trading systems or electronic communication networks as "electronic trading systems that automatically match buy and sell orders at specified prices."[5] The SEC describes ECNs as integral to modern securities markets. Several ECNs are currently registered in the NASDAQ system, which includes Archipelago, BRASS, Instinet, and Island. ECNs' automated communication and matching systems have led to lower trading costs.

There are currently five major ECNs according to the TABB Group: Instinet (INET), Bloomberg (TradeBook), Archipelago (ArcaEx), SunGard (Brut), and NASDAQ's own SuperMontage. Each of these ECNs is a liquidity pool that houses its own order books. Traditionally, an order will search its own liquidity pool before routing an order to a competing ECN. This could mean that there may be a more advantageous order waiting at another ECN, but the order will not execute against the more profitable order because it has been matched within the trader's initial parameters within the ECN. This has caused fragmentation in U.S. equity markets where liquidity in one venue does not interact or interacts poorly with other market pools. To counteract this fragmentation, firms and technology vendors have developed aggregation tools or DMA technology.

---

[4] Adam Sussman, *Institutional Equity Trading in America: A Buy-Side Perspective,* TABB Group Annual Industry Research Study, June 2005: 38–41.

[5] U.S. Securities and Exchange Commission, "Electronic Communication Networks," http://www.sec.gov/answers/ecn.htm.

Crossing networks are a method of accessing liquidity from other sources that may not be readily available in an active market. They allow institutions to efficiently trade large orders in illiquid stocks. Crossing networks have increased in popularity in recent years as the buy side's difficulty in executing block trades has increased (see Exhibit 7.3). One of the few places where large blocks can be efficiently executed with low market impact is through a crossing network.

There are a number of different matching models for crossing networks. According to the TABB Group, Posit, Instinet Crossing, and the NASDAQ Open and Close use a scheduled crossing model. In a scheduled crossing model, orders in the system are anonymous to participants, and unmatched orders can be canceled, retained to await the next match, or routed to another real-time market for matching. The next model, called continuous crossing, provides access to liquidity and negotiations throughout the day. The continuous model provides more information and hence is prone to information leakage. The third model is called the dark box model. This is a hybrid between the continuous and scheduled models. This allows firms to hide liquidity in the dark box, providing price improvement to both sides without the broadcast of any information. Crossing networks have increased their market penetration in recent years, lifting the volume of the leading providers. This change in positioning highlights the growing importance of anonymity to buy-side traders.

ECNs can typically provide the following information:

1. Security identification
2. Buy or sell order

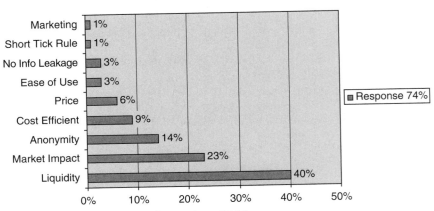

The Appeal of Crossing Networks

Exhibit 7.3   *Source:* TABB Group, June 2005.

3. Trade price
4. Trade date
5. Order instruction (i.e., market, limit, or crossed order)
6. Style classifications of the institutions
7. Broker identification

Broker-dealers have traditionally been the gatekeepers to the securities transfer infrastructure. Investors previously required the services of an introducing broker to channel their trades through an exchange. ECNs are not legally restricted from exchange access and can provide transactions to a wider group of investors. ECNs can match buyers and sellers directly; they have bypassed human intermediaries, reducing their profits. ECNs offer more efficient order execution than established market centers' trading systems. ECNs provide liquidity for investors with more complete price information by allowing them to see the ECN's limit order book. Nevertheless, despite the electronic trading system's proven advantages, many traders have still not welcomed ECNs (see Exhibit 7.4). Traders claim that large orders cannot be executed efficiently on ECNs and that executing through ECNs conflicts with the immediacy required to execute before an anticipated market move. Contrary to this belief, ECNs can effectively execute large orders through rapid-fire small, block trades as brokers and market makers do today, but can also offer anonymity. Buy-side and sell-side traders seek order anonymity in the market. In traditional trading, the identity of the firm, the size of the firm, and its trading practices are all known by the intermediary chosen to execute an order for a buy-side client. That same intermediary usually has a relationship with at least 200 other high-commission-paying firms. ECNs, however, are the very definition

Percentage of Buy-Side Traders Using ECNs

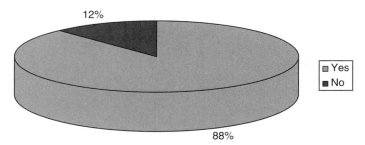

Exhibit 7.4   *Source: LLC Institutional Equity Trading in America*, TABB Group, April 2004.

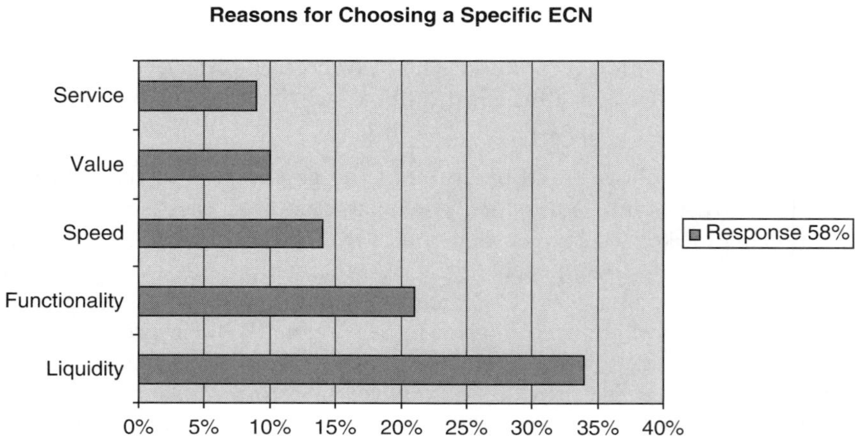

Reasons for Choosing a Specific ECN

Service	
Value	
Speed	▣ Response 58%
Functionality	
Liquidity	

0%   5%   10%   15%   20%   25%   30%   35%   40%

Exhibit 7.5   *Source: LLC Institutional Equity Trading in America*, TABB Group, April 2004.

of anonymity in trading. Buy-side traders prefer to trade large blocks of stock because blocks are easier to account for and to book. The typical viewpoint is that block trades cannot be executed on ECNs; however, ECNs for listed trades and orders are highly visible and tend to attract the other side of the order more easily (see Exhibit 7.5).

ECNs can display only price and size of order, offering anonymity and stealth for traders and investors. When an ECN can find an internal match, the trades execute immediately. When internal matches cannot be found, an ECN can offer subscribers the option to leave the limit order on the ECN, or route the order to another market.

ECNs compete with one another by targeting different clientele or following different strategies. Some ECNs only utilize limit orders or are destination-only, meaning that orders do not leave the ECN until they are canceled, regardless of whether or not the trade may be executed elsewhere. Other ECNs take market orders and if an internal match is not available, route it to NASDAQ in search of the optimal price.

ECNs offer services that can access multiple markets or different products. This can be handled through proprietary methods or algorithms selecting the market venue that is likely to provide the best combination of speed, quality, price, and certainty of execution for customers. ECNs charge fees that include fixed components such as cost of purchasing a terminal and line feed, and a per-share fee for execution. Other ECN subscribers submit limit orders with no charge and pay an access fee for orders that execute against a standing ECN limit order.

7.4 Shifting Trends

Investment firms are beginning to significantly reallocate the way they route their orders in response to different interdependent forces. Lower commissions and access to liquidity allow for better investment performance. Regulatory pressures struggle to improve best execution parameters such as market impact and price. Brokers and technology providers are offering better and more integrated technologies to both access and to utilize low-touch trading strategies. Overall, buy-side firms have routed less order flow to phones and are increasing their trade executions through FIX-based flow (see Exhibit 7.6).

In the transition from phone-based orders to utilizing FIX, buy-side traders can shift their attention to less menial tasks. Asset management firms can reduce the overall cost of trading. In the shift from sales desks to technology channels such as ECNs, DMAs, algorithms, and crossing, the winners of this liquidity shift will be developers of algorithmic solutions, DMA and ECN platform providers, and other alternative trading venues that will come at the expense of the broker's traditional sales desk (see Exhibit 7.7). The most significant order flow shift in recent years has occurred in large firms; however, smaller and medium-size firms also plan on participating. The long-term effects of the liquidity shift are beginning to be felt as brokers, exchanges, and financial technology providers develop business strategies for the more independent and electronically oriented trader.

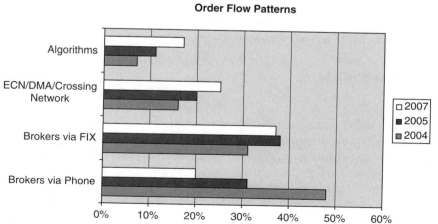

Order Flow Patterns

Exhibit 7.6 *Source:* TABB Group, June 2005.

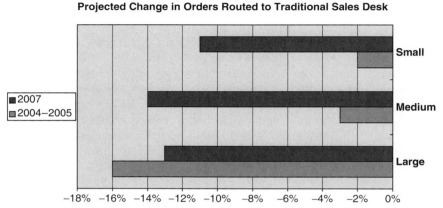

Exhibit 7.7   *Source:* TABB Group, June 2005.

THE IMPORTANCE OF DMA

The buy side has been taking more control of its trading decisions while looking for faster, lower-cost, anonymous executions. DMA tools permit buy-side traders to access liquidity pools and multiple execution venues directly without intervention from a broker's trading desk. DMA has been rapidly adopted by institutional traders in order to aggregate liquidity. Hedge funds are among the most aggressive users of DMA. In 2004, Banc of America Securities bought Direct Financial Access Corp.; BNY Brokerage purchased Sonic Financial Technologies; and Citigroup acquired Lava Trading. DMAs have become commoditized for bulge-bracket firms as part of a comprehensive set of services encompassing DMA, program trading, and traditional block trading.

7.5 Conclusion

The buy side has begun to take more control of its trading decisions through faster, lower-cost, anonymous executions. The growth of communication networks such as ECNs has developed alternative trading platforms associated with more tightly quoted, effective bid-ask spreads, greater depth, and less concentrated markets. As a result, the increase in ECN trading has caused some traditional market makers to exit the industry or has caused them to adapt. Institutional broker dealers have rapidly adopted direct market access as a method of aggregating liquidity fragmented across U.S. execution venues. Buy-side customers under regulatory pressure are also seeking best execution and greater control over their trading strategies. As of 2005, the cost of executing a trade through direct market access was about one cent a share, while program trades cost roughly two cents a share and block trades cost four to five cents. Thirty-three percent of buy-side equity shares were routed via DMA as of 2004, and 38 percent of buy-side shares will be executed through DMA by 2008 according to estimates made by TowerGroup.[6] Broker-dealers are scrambling to differentiate their services, expanding their DMA coverage beyond equities into fixed income. Broker-dealers have been acquiring independent DMA vendors in order to remain competitive. Broker-dealers and investment banks have been encompassing DMA technology, leveraging it through program trading, traditional block trading, and transaction cost analysis services on top of DMA offerings. For a broker-dealer, the costs associated with building DMA trading capabilities from scratch are around $15 million. A large bulge-bracket firm may spend $50 million, according to the TABB Group.

---

[6] Ivy Schmerken, "Direct Market Access Trading," *Finance Tech*, February 4, 2005.

Chapter 8

Effective Data Management

8.1 Introduction

The ability to collect and disseminate massive amounts of market data has allowed traders to execute transactions through an algorithm based on established sets of trading parameters. The speed at which market data can be processed can mean the difference between a successful or unsuccessful trade. Milliseconds (1/1,000 of a second) can cost a firm an opportunity to profit from a trade. According to the Securities Industry Automation Corp (SIAC), message traffic for data is growing quickly. Compare these numbers reported for sustained 1-minute peak messages per second in the month of November during the last three years:

- November 2004: 56,000 messages per second
- November 2005: 121,000 messages per second
- November 2006: ~200,000 messages per second

Every firm that utilizes algorithmic trading is looking for ways to reduce message transmission delays and attain zero latency. Market data providers constantly work to provide more efficient flow of data, but eliminating the data provider completely and linking feeds directly from the source and aggregating the data will further delay transmission of information.

8.2 Real-Time Data

The ability to process massive amounts of real-time and historical data for quantitative analysis has become a clear advantage for the development of algorithmic trading. Data flow into both the buy side and the sell side has increased exponentially; a fully integrated database solution must be established to facilitate real-time analysis. The increase in the number of transactions and the speed at which data can be now processed has had a major impact on the financial industry. This increase is forcing broker-dealers and investment firms to invest significantly in updating their trading and processing infrastructure. As speeds increase, market data infrastructures will be the first to sag. A more sophisticated trading infrastructure will see substantial investments in risk management and product integration. The increase in the volume and number of transactions is due to increases in liquidity, and new trading techniques such as algorithmic trading, which gives traders the ability to execute larger and larger orders without moving the market. Sophisticated analytics and high-speed connectivity allow traders to split up large orders into small executable shares. The challenges in the future will be to update underlying infrastructure such as faster servers, enhanced networking technology in a more cost-conscious environment. The challenges firms will face include enhancing and analyzing real-time data efficiently while maintaining a low-cost infrastructure because real-time processing will also lower margins, cost structures, and competitive barriers.

New technologies such as algorithmic and black box trading have not only increased the number of trades and reduced the number of shares per trade, but have also changed the dynamics of market data such as the ability to record and replicate trading patterns for canceled orders. According to the TABB Group, this is pushing market data speeds through the roof with tick volumes beginning to push 2,000 to 3,000 ticks per minute for highly liquid securities. The TABB Group estimates that algorithmic or black box trading strategies comprise 6% of all order flow for equities (see Exhibit 8.1). Should black box strategies begin to account for 60–70% of all order flow in the future, the tick count may increase seven- to tenfold. While these trading models may potentially enhance trading performance, many investment managers think they do not offer a true competitive advantage because clients cannot change, manipulate, or observe how the strategy works. Traders now see strategy enablers through predeveloped models catered to their specific needs.[1]

---

[1] Larry Tabb, *Pushing the Envelope: Redefining Real-Time Transaction Processing in Financial Markets*, TABB Group Report, March 2004, http://www.tabbgroup.com/our_reports .php?tabbaction=4&reportId=51.

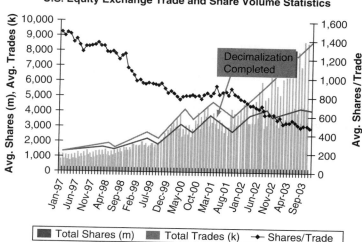

Exhibit 8.1 *Source:* NYSE, NASDAQ, Cincinnati Stock Exchange, and ArcaEx, *Data: The Life Blood of the New Electronic Marketplace*, TABB Group, April 2005.

8.3 Strategy Enablers

A new category of technology enablers has emerged to assist in the development of analytics. These enablers assist clients as a foundation for analyzing massive amounts of data to develop new or modify existing algorithms. These platforms are also configured for developing pre- and post-trade analytics through real-time and historical data.

ORDER MANAGEMENT SYSTEMS

The following list gives examples of several key features to assist in executing an algorithmic trade, according to the Aite Group:

- **Trade blotter**   A trade blotter functions as the central hub, enabling traders to manage orders/lists, apply various benchmarks on the fly, and keep track of current positions, execution data, confirmations, and real-time P&L.
- **Prepackaged algorithms**   Most firms now offer prepackaged algorithms (e.g., pairs, long/short, ETF arbitrage, VWAP, risk arbitrage, etc.) designed to attract those smaller firms that lack algorithm-building

capability. The key to prepackaged algorithms is to ensure that they are flexible enough to enable modification and customization by the clients.

- **Pre- and post-trade analytics** Pre-trade analytics can help traders determine which algorithm is most suitable given a certain trading situation, as well as estimate cost for a given trade. Post-trade analytics in turn can be used to measure trading performance, benchmarks, and other firm-established trading parameters.
- **FIX connectivity** FIX is the lifeline of algorithmic trading systems as connectivity to various market participants and various market venues enables the system to make timely trading decisions driven by algorithms (see Exhibit 8.2).
- **Handling multiple asset classes** Algorithmic trading systems should be able to go beyond just equities in terms of financial products supported. A typical system currently handles fixed income, derivatives, FX, and so on.
- **Compliance and regulatory reporting** Similar to single stock/block trading order management systems, algorithmic trading systems must be able to accommodate the constantly changing regulatory environment of the U.S. securities industry through customizable, rules-based compliance triggers and flexible reporting capability.

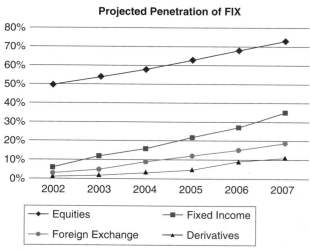

Exhibit 8.2   *Source:* Aite Group estimates.

8.4 Order Routing

Once the pre-trade analytics have been determined, and the decision has been made as to what to trade and when, the next decision is to figure out what type of orders and through what execution venue to route orders that meet the parameters set by the trading strategy. Order routing is also the domain of direct market access technology providers. Some of the key functionality of direct access platforms includes the following:

- Consolidated view of various execution points
- Full view (market data) and access to multiple levels of liquidity across different execution venues
- Ability to sweep across multiple execution venues, tapping into hidden, reserve liquidity discreetly and rapidly to minimize market impact
- Connectivity to all major execution venues
- Full historical audit trail for post-trade analysis and compliance requirements

TRADE VOLUME

Today's trading systems must constantly evaluate market conditions because the influence of speed, frequency, and velocity of data has never been greater. They can evaluate dynamic market conditions up to tens of thousands of times per second for thousands of unique stocks that have as many as 50 ticks per second and several times more for options, while they seek to exploit short-term intraday trading opportunities. The growth is so rapid that the Options Price Reporting Authority (OPRA) states that the required capacity had grown to 173,000 messages per second by the summer of 2006. OPRA provides quote and trade data from the six U.S. options exchanges. According to the Financial Information Forum, a centralized information bureau for the U.S. equities and options market run by the Securities Industry Automation Corp (SIAC), message traffic peaked at 121,000 messages per second in November 2005. As of the summer of 2006, anyone getting a direct OPRA feed must be able to handle a peak messaging rate of 173,000 per second or 1.3 billion messages daily. This has risen from 53,000 per second at the end of 2004 (see Exhibit 8.3).

OPTIMIZING DATA INFRASTRUCTURE

The TABB Group estimates that the global securities industry spends nearly $4 billion on real-time market data, updating their electronic trading infrastructure and meeting requirements for compliance. There are

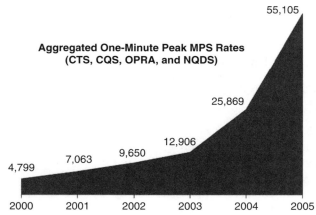

Exhibit 8.3   Messages per second. *Source:* Robert Iati, SIAC, OPRA, and NAS-DAQ, *Data: The Life Blood of the New Electronic Marketplace*, TABB Group, April 2005.

numerous players in the algorithmic trading market, ranging from bulge-bracket firms and large agency brokers to small technology-driven technology providers. As the market speeds up and more volume flows through the broker's electronic infrastructure, the importance of real-time risk management infrastructure increases. Many hedge funds and institutional investors leverage the broker's execution infrastructure so the broker becomes liable for problems stemming from their client's trading. Regulators must analyze massive amounts of market activity in real time, seeking to recognize patterns that identify illegal trading behavior. New development in a brokerage firm's trading system requires at least equal development in its surveillance system. However, most financial services institutions do not have the ability to reach an optimal infrastructure because resources for most of a brokerage firm's cost center have fallen victim to applying discretionary funds within the profit center such as the trading area of the business. It is clearly evident that budgets for data infrastructure have been reduced in the past years when the need for enhancing performance and technology has never been greater. Presumably, this will change in the future, though, when linking data to trading profitability becomes more evident.

8.5 Impact on Operations and Technology

Real-time transaction processing and electronic trading can result in a great deal of automation for operations. Real-time transactions move more quickly, tend to be more accurate, have fewer problems, and need less attention than manually engaged transactions. According to the TABB Group, 60% of trades were processed manually over seven years ago. Now, highly automated firms can process 75% of trades automatically. The other 25% of trades tend to be either the most complex or most profitable. Firms have also considered outsourcing their back office in order to eliminate overhead in the process that it takes to settle unprofitable or problematic trades. Other factors are increasing the drive to automate trade settlement. The increasing volume in trades and large block orders being sliced into numerous smaller trades creates a need to more efficiently allocate, confirm, and process the transactions. The settlement process is expected to move to real time in the future, but this is highly unlikely to occur until the industry as a whole moves toward a T+1 settlement cycle. The push to speed up financing, prime brokerage services, and more aggressive trading techniques will all become a motivational factor for firms to upgrade their clearance and settlement infrastructure.

The impact of real-time transaction processing will not only require firms to upgrade their infrastructure, but also require the cooperation of industry participants, exchanges, and vendors in order to facilitate the increase in trade volume, market data, and post-trade activity. The NASDAQ, for example, has decentralized its infrastructure to manage high-speed electronic trading while the NYSE is eliminating specialists to increase liquidity. This will require significant upgrades to the NYSE infrastructure, however. In addition to exchanges, pre- and post-trade utilities such as the Consolidated Tape Association (CTA), the Depository Trust & Clearing Corporation (DTCC), and the Securities Industry Automation Corporation (SIAC) will need to respond to this increase in traffic as will major industry vendors such as ADP, SunGard, and Thomson.

8.6 Conclusion

The drive for attaining faster market data will provide an advantage for algorithmic trading providers. Eventually, this will hit an apex where market data cannot be disseminated any faster. When that focal point is reached, the quality and reliability of data will begin to play a crucial role in determining the success of an algorithmic trade. The ability to design systems that can better process and analyze market data will eventually differentiate the performance of a specific algorithm.

Chapter 9

Minimizing Execution Costs

9.1 Introduction

An optimal trading strategy begins with the accurate measurement of trading costs and implementation shortfall. André Perold defines implementation shortfall as the difference in return between a theoretical portfolio and the implemented portfolio. In a paper portfolio, a portfolio manager looks at prevailing prices, in relation to execution prices in an actual portfolio. Implementation shortfall measures the price distance between the final, realized trade price, and a pre-trade decision price.[1] A trade not only executes an investment idea, but the trader must also envision effective transaction cost management. The idea of a potential trade must forecast expected trading costs to be incorporated into an optimized portfolio, and then measure post-trade performance. An institutional trader must manage a portfolio manager's or model's expectations and gauge the reality of the market and implicit transaction costs. The ultimate goal is to execute, meet, or exceed expectations with your forecast, measurement, and management ability.

Perold's metric is the sum of four components:

$$\text{Implementation Shortfall} = \text{Cost due to manager's delay} + \text{Explicit costs} \\ + \text{Implicit costs} + \text{Opportunity costs}$$

---

[1] André F. Perold, "The Implementation Shortfall: Paper vs. Reality," *Journal of Portfolio Management* 14, no. 3 (Spring 1988).

Measuring trading costs entails looking at bid-ask spread, price impacts with liquidity, management style with different market trends, cost of waiting and commissions, fees, and taxes also known as explicit costs. The cost due to a bid-ask spread, or implicit cost, is generally calculated as a spread between the best ask price and best bid price available in the market. Portfolio managers will trade only to the extent that the expected value of the information is greater than the costs incurred to gather the information and implement the trades.

9.2 Components of Trading Costs

BID-ASK SPREAD

The bid-ask spread is the price at which an investor or money manager can purchase an asset (the dealer's ask price) and the price at which you can sell the same asset at the same point in time (the dealer's bid price). The price impact this usually creates by trading an asset pushes up the price when buying an asset and pushes it down while selling. Long-term investment strategies are made by portfolio managers. They make clear decisions about what to buy, sell, and hold. In a study conducted by the Zero Alpha Group surveying a consortium of financial advisers, the average annual trading cost for a mutual fund was 0.27% or $27 on a $10,000 investment. Table 9.1 shows a sample population of the five funds that have the highest brokerage costs.

The widespread use of fund investment objectives that classify fund types can differentiate trading costs. Aggressive growth funds, for example, can potentially have higher average costs than more conservative growth and income funds. Virtually all equity managers suggest that paper portfolios outperform real ones. A paper portfolio is an imaginary holding consisting of all the security positions the investor decides to hold, acquired at the

**Table 9.1   Trading Costs as a Percentage
of Net Assets**

Fund	Trading Costs
Fidelity	1.06%
Fidelity Contrafund	0.80%
Putnam Voyager A	0.80%
Fidelity Equity-Income II	0.79%
AIM Constellation A	0.47%

Source: The Zero Alpha Group.

midquote price that prevailed at the time the manager decided to hold them. Paper portfolios incur no commissions, no taxes, no bid-ask spreads, no market impact, and no opportunity costs. Real portfolios incur all of these costs. The performance of an actual portfolio compared to the performance of a hypothetical paper portfolio in which trades are made at notional "benchmark" prices is the difference between notional prices and trades that consider implementation costs. Common benchmark prices for trades are the midpoint for the bid and ask quotes prevailing at the time the decision was made to invest (the bid-ask midpoint is abbreviated as BAM).

The following examples compare an actual portfolio versus a theoretical portfolio traded at notional "benchmark prices":

- In an actual portfolio, the portfolio manager decides to buy 100 shares of ABC stock. The market is 50 bid, 51 offer. Trader buys at 51.20, paying $29 commission:

  Cash outflow $= 5,120 + 29 = 5,149$

- When the portfolio manager decides to sell, the market is 54 bid, 54.50 offer. Trader sells at 54, paying $29 commission:

  Cash inflow $= 5,400 - 29 = 5,371$

- Net cash flow is $5,371 - 5,149 = 222$ (4.31% return).
- In a theoretical portfolio, the buy and sell are at the midpoint of the bid and ask spread at time of purchase.
- One hundred shares are purchased at 50.50 (midpoint of 50 bid 51 offer) and sold at 54.25 (midpoint of 54 bid 54.50 offer) $= 375$ (7.43% return).
- Ignoring all interest costs, no bid-ask spreads, but simple midpoint price utilization and opportunity cost, this portfolio's return is 7.43% vs. 4.31% in the actual scenario.
- The initial purchase was made $0.70 per share above the BAM, and the final sale was made $0.25 per share below the BAM.
- The implicit cost (cost of interacting with the market) with respect to the BAM is the effective cost. The effective cost (see Exhibit 9.1) is a useful measure for market orders.

9.3 Price Impacts with Liquidity

Price impacts usually occur because markets are not completely liquid. Large trades can create imbalances between buy and sell orders. Price changes occur from a lack of liquidity and are generally temporary and reversed when liquidity returns to the market. Price impacts are usually

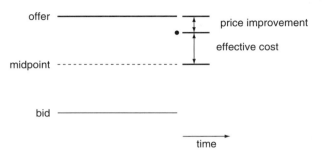

Exhibit 9.1   *Source*: Joel Hasbrouck, "Introduction to Trading Objectives, Costs, and Strategies," November 2002.

informational. Large trades attract other investors in that market because they might be motivated by new information that the trader may possess. While investors may be wrong on the informational value of large block trades, there is also reason to believe that they will be right almost as often.

The variables that determine the price impact of trading are the same variables driving the bid-ask spread. The price impact and the bid-ask spread are both a function of the liquidity of the market. The inventory costs and adverse selection problems are likely to be largest for stocks where small trades can move the market significantly. The difference between the price at which an investor can buy the asset and the price at which one can sell, at the same point in time, is a reflection of both the bid-ask spread and the expected price impact of the trade on the asset. This difference can theoretically be very large in markets where trading is infrequent; this cost may amount to more than 20% of the value of the asset in certain markets. The size of the portfolio can be a critical aspect of price impact. The largest portfolios usually trade the largest blocks, which have the biggest price impact.

Thomas Loeb[2] predicted that transaction cost in percentage of value as a function of trade size is a percentage of outstanding shares and market capitalization. A sample size of 13,651 equity purchases was used totaling nearly $2 billion made by a large U.S. corporate pension plan in 1991 to test this theory. The study was conducted by the Plexus Group, which analyzed

---

[2] Thomas Loeb, "Is There a Gift for Small Stock Investing?" *Financial Analysts Journal*, January–February 1991: 39–44.

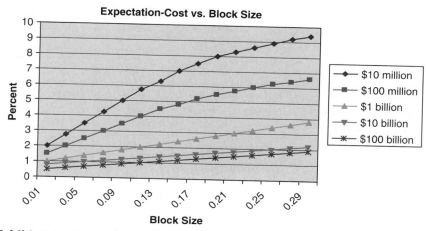

Exhibit 9.2 *Source:* David J. Leinweber, *Trading and Portfolio Management: Ten Years Later*, California Institute of Technology, May 2002.

transaction costs, with the cooperation of a fund manager providing data. Trade sizes ranged from 100 shares to blocks of more than 400,000 shares. Exhibit 9.2 shows the predictions of what is expected.

COSTS AND MANAGEMENT STYLE

Can transaction costs be predicted through investment management style? Patient disciplines such as value and growth investing with longer time horizons may be expected to have lower transaction costs. Investment strategies that depend on quicker execution to capture the market's reaction to differences between expected and actual earnings may have higher transactions. Index funds tracking small capitalization stocks would theoretically be expected to have larger transaction costs because of the characteristics of smaller stock made up in those indexes. The theoretical expectations are shown in Exhibit 9.3. However, the actual observations are listed in Exhibit 9.4.

Why is there such a wide deviation between the expectations summarized versus the actual observations? Several explanations can be made regarding the results. Investment managers and traders executing on behalf of disciplines focused on value and growth with long-term horizons may lack the skill-set to be savvy enough to execute at the best available execution price.

Management Style	Trade Motivation	Liquidity Demands	Execution Costs	Opportunity Costs
Value	Value	Low	Low	Low
Growth	Value	Low	Low	Low
Earnings Surprise	Information	High	High	High
Index-Fund Large-Cap	Passive	Variable	Variable	High
Index-Fund Small-Cap	Passive	High	High	High

Exhibit 9.3 Expectations—cost and management style. *Source:* David J. Leinweber, *Trading and Portfolio Management: Ten Years Later*, California Institute of Technology, May 2002.

These traders may lack close relationships with the street to get the best prices through comparison shopping. Traders executing on behalf of investment strategies that depend on quick execution based on market reaction may have better relationships with broker-dealers who may offer price discounts to give incentive for quick execution traders to come back and

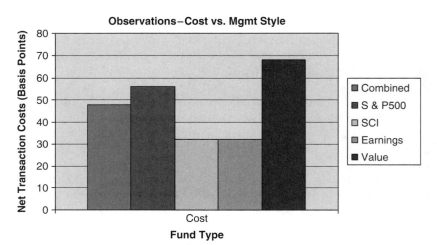

Exhibit 9.4 *Source:* David J. Leinweber, *Trading and Portfolio Management: Ten Years Later*, California Institute of Technology, May 2002.

generate more business for them. They may also have a better understanding of market trends, and trade on volume generating more business for brokers, giving them more bargaining power to find the best execution price.

9.4 Cost of Waiting

Large block trades affect bid-ask spread and have consequences with price impacts. However, there is a cost of waiting, which prevents large investors from breaking up trades into small lots or buying and selling large quantities without affecting the price or spread significantly. The penalties relating to the cost of waiting occur when investors wait to buy, but at a higher price, reducing expected profits from the investment; or when the price, of the asset rises significantly to the point that the asset becomes overvalued.

The factors determining the cost of waiting include the following:[3]

- Whether or not the valuation assessment is based upon private information or is based on public information. Private information tends to have a short shelf life in financial markets, and the risks of sitting on private information are much greater than the risks of waiting when the valuation assessment is based upon public information. The cost of waiting is much larger when the strategy is to buy on rumors of a possible takeover than it would be in a strategy of buying low PE ratio stocks.
- Whether or not other investors are actively seeking the same information in the market. When an investor possesses valuable information, the risk of waiting is much greater in markets where other investors are actively searching the same information.
- Whether or not the investment strategy is short- or long-term. Short-term strategies are much more likely to be affected by the cost of waiting than longer-term strategies. This can be attributed to the fact that short-term strategies are more likely to be motivated by private information, whereas long-term strategies are more likely to be motivated by views on value.
- Whether or not the investment strategy is a "contrarian" or "momentum" strategy. In a contrarian strategy, investors are investing against the prevailing tide; the cost of waiting is likely to be smaller because of this behavior. The cost of waiting in a "momentum" strategy is likely to be higher since the investor is buying when other investors are selling

[3] Aswath Damodaran, "Trading Cost and Taxes," pp. 17–20, http://pages.stern.nyu.edu/~adamodar/pdfiles/invphiloh/tradingcosts.pdf.

and vice versa. Traders with superior information earn abnormal returns that just offset their opportunity and implementation costs. This implies that the portfolio return should on average offset the fees and trading costs imposed by the investment manager.

9.5 Explicit Costs—Commissions, Fees, and Taxes

Commissions, fees, and taxes are unavoidable costs and can significantly alter a fund or stock's portfolio. Taxes are important because some investment strategies expose investors to a much greater tax liability than other strategies (see Exhibit 9.5). A fund with a long-term horizon philosophy may have lower transaction costs as well as lower tax implications. Funds that trade frequently may be affected by higher taxes. An accurate measure of an investment strategy is observing after-tax returns and not pre-tax returns.

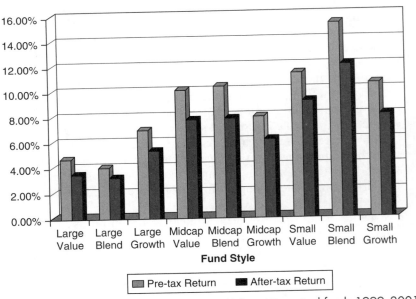

Exhibit 9.5   Pre-tax and after-tax returns at U.S. equity mutual funds 1999–2001. *Source:* Aswath Damodaran, "Trading Cost and Taxes," p. 30, http://pages.stern. nyu.edu/~adamodar/pdfiles/invphiloh/tradingcosts.pdf.

The Evolution of Trading Strategies to Minimize Transaction Costs

The development of sophisticated technology has changed the way we access markets and trade stocks. New order-routing technologies, algorithm strategies, and alternative trading venues are shifting the responsibility for best execution from traditional brokers to money managers themselves. The trend in financial markets today is the increasing use of computer trading, which offers a specific benchmark. Quality can be more easily measured with trading performance. This phenomenon is explained through the accessibility of execution systems previously only available to sell-side traders. Now these systems are becoming more recently available to clients via electronic platforms or electronic communication networks. The Volume-Weighted Average Price, commonly known as VWAP, is becoming the most familiar trade benchmark. The computation of a daily VWAP is straightforward for anyone with access to records of daily stock transactions. Simply add up the dollars traded for every transaction (price times shares traded) and then divide by the total shares traded for the day. The use of VWAP to judge trading is simplicity itself: If the price of a buy trade is lower than the VWAP, it is a good trade. If the price is higher, it is a bad trade. For a sell trade, the valuation is reversed. The use of new order-routing technologies and trade benchmarking such as the VWAP is steadily dropping transaction rates and forcing broker-dealers to become more efficient in processing trades and leaning on automation along with computer power to cut costs. Firms are increasingly looking to outsource their trading desks to increase their capacity and to execute more volume. Brokerage commissions are at an all-time low, and a general reduction in trading personnel in favor of advanced electronic resources is further driving down transaction costs.

Transaction cost research will play an increasingly important role in selecting the proper algorithm integrated with an order management system. Buy-side traders and money managers will view transaction cost research as another critical piece in making a trading decision with their national best bid or offer. The need to curb transaction costs and market impact for high-volume trades, direct market access, and front-end automation is starting to converge. Buy-side firms such as hedge funds are now starting to have greater access to algorithms from brokers via an order management system, as well as algorithmic trading capabilities provided by third-party software companies.

The heightened scrutiny of best execution in the United States may help explain the declining cost of trading even as most of the world's financial markets become more expensive. The increased emphasis on efficiency has spurred growth such as agency-only brokerage firms relying solely on computerized algorithms to execute trades. According to the Aite Group, 50% of all U.S. institutional trades are now handled in some low-touch methods or in trades that can be automatically processed and executed with little or no human intervention. Twenty percent of all volume comes from program trades at a cut-rate commission. Slightly fewer trades, approximately 18%, are being handled by a direct market access system. A direct market access (DMA) provides buy-side traders with simultaneous connectivity to multiple markets and allows big orders to be split up. Twelve percent of transactions are being handled by an algorithmic platform, which combines the features of a DMA system, parceling out pieces of orders among different destinations over time to minimize implicit costs.

The bulk of U.S. cost reductions come from lower commissions, which fell from 17.83 basis points to 14.81 basis points for NYSE stocks and from 21.19 basis points to 16.67 basis points for NASDAQ shares. The next biggest component of all in costs, market impact, actually rose by a slight margin over the past year on those two markets. The significant reduction in commission costs and the increased use of DMA, program trading, algorithmic systems, and crossing networks are cutting into the traditional "high-touch" brokerage business that charged a nickel per share to transact business.

9.6 Conclusion

True transaction costs are fundamentally immeasurable. This is because they are the difference between the price you paid and the price that would have prevailed if you had not transacted. We can never observe this price, so we can never measure true costs. The implementation shortfall method has been widely accepted as a good surrogate measure for true transaction costs.[4] The minimization of market impact, efficiently finding sources of liquidity anonymously, and the need to achieve best execution for low- or no-touch trading strategy can be addressed through the use of an algorithm.

Examples of common algorithmic trading strategies that can improve trading costs for buy-side firms include enhanced DMA strategies:

1. **Iceberging** A large order that can be partially hidden from other market participants by specifying a maximum number of shares to be shown.

---

[4] David J. Leinweber, "Trading and Portfolio Management: Ten Years Later" (Working Paper Series 1135, California Institute of Technology, Div. Humanities & Social Sciences, May 2002: 5–6), http://www.hss.caltech.edu/SSPapers/wp1135.pdf.

2. **Pegging** An order sent out at the best bid (ask) if buying (selling), and if the price moves, the order is modified accordingly.
3. **Smart order routing** Mainly a U.S. phenomenon—liquidity from many different sources is aggregated and orders are sent out to the destination offering the best price or liquidity.
4. **Simple time slicing** The order is split up and market orders are sent at regular time intervals.
5. **Simple market on close (MOC)** The order is sent into the closing auction.

Other common algorithmic trading strategies include quantitative algorithms:

1. **VWAP** Attempts to minimize tracking error while maximizing performance versus the Volume-Weighted Average Price. Similar to simple time slicing, but aims to minimize spread and impact costs.
2. **TWAP** Aims to match the Time-Weighted Average Price. Similar to simple time slicing, but aims to minimize spread and impact costs.
3. **Participate** Also known as Inline, Follow, With Volume, POV. Aims to be a user-specified fraction of the volume traded in the market.
4. **MOC** Enhanced MOC strategy that optimizes risk and impact, possibly starting trading before the closing auction.
5. **Implementation shortfall or arrival price** Manages the trade-off between impact and risk to execute as close as possible to the midpoint when the order is entered.[5]

---

[5] Tom Middleton, "Understanding How Algorithms Work," in *Algorithmic Trading: A Buy-Side Handbook*, 22–23 (London: The Trade Ltd., 2005).

Chapter 10

Transaction Cost Research

10.1 Introduction

New technologies, such as utilizing algorithms and straight-through processing, result from the drive to lower transaction costs, as well as the associated research involved behind each execution. According to the TABB Group, Transaction Cost Research (TCR) is defined as the amount of money spent to open a new position or to close an existing position. Transaction cost analysis started with fulfilling regulatory requirements. It can significantly drag performance, especially for portfolio strategies that include high turn-over. All transactions have explicit and implicit costs. Explicit costs are disclosed prior to the trade and include commissions, markups, and other fees. Implicit costs represent the costs that are not determined until after the execution of a trade or set of trades is completed. TCR can be defined as the movement of the stock price from the time of the investment decision to the expiration or completion of the order. Minimizing implicit cost is a key factor in gauging execution quality. Commissions are generated through trade execution; however, commissions fund multiple services, which include execution, research, conferences, and technology. Transaction costs affect investors, pension plans, money managers, and broker-dealers. These costs are ultimately passed on to the investor. TCR includes the measurement of transaction costs after the trade is executed (post-trade) as well as expected costs before the order is placed (pre-trade).[1] As investment

---

[1] Adam Sussman, *From Best Ex to Coaching*, TABB Group Report, June 2005, http://www.tabbgroup.com/our_reports.php?tabbaction=4&reportId=105.

management becomes increasingly competitive, portfolio managers will look for methods of enhancing their returns through lower transaction costs to boost their overall rate of return. On the contrary, broker-dealers and the sell side will try to adapt and continue to service the investment community through lowering commissions and transaction costs by routing executions via electronic venues such as direct market access (DMA) or algorithms (see Exhibit 10.1).

Brokers are under enormous pressure to reduce brokerage commissions. This has caused profit margins to fall, and research costs become increasingly paid for by the broker. The push by the buy side to segment commissions and transaction costs between research and trading led to Fidelity's landmark deal with Lehman Brothers. Fidelity agreed to pay approximately $7 million USD annually for research and approximately 0.02–0.025 cents per share for execution services. Large buy-side investment managers such as Fidelity already have their own research staff, and would most likely put further pressure to segment and lower sell-side research and trading costs with other broker-dealers. Some money managers pay for research out of their own pocket (hard dollars) and receive lower commission costs, translating to higher management fees. Other investment managers may combine research and execution commissions paying higher rates. Firms with limited research needs may use DMA and algorithms. Electronic and algorithmic trading has been one avenue that has helped sell-side firms to retain order flow and lower transaction costs, but they lack a solid method of retaining relationships with the investment community.

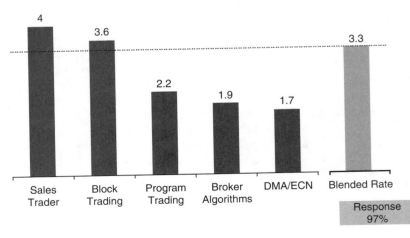

Per-Share Commission Cost by Execution/Per-Share Commission Cost by Execution Venue (in pennies)

Exhibit 10.1 *Source:* TABB Group.

10.2 Post-Trade TCR

Regulatory reporting for executions required by the exchanges and the NASD has led to a wealth of trade data and new software data providers willing to provide this information. Due to these reasons, post-trade analysis was developed prior to pre-trade analysis. The data used to research post-trade analysis include commissions, market data, and the attributes of the order. After the data is collected, the analysis attempts to piece together the transaction costs and determine their origin. The more detailed the information, the more precise the analysis can be. A high-level overview may show how the trade's execution compares to a particular benchmark, or ideal price. A more detailed analysis goes beyond calculating transaction costs and attempts to show when the costs were incurred or why it happened.

Post-trade analytics face many sets of challenges (see Exhibit 10.2). One of the biggest problems the buy side faces is methodology and flawed measurements. Critical data such as historical volatility, liquidity constraints, and adjustments for various market capitalizations are not being included in transaction cost calculations. Post-trade analytics can also be inaccurate, which impacts adoption rates. Another issue is selecting the appropriate benchmark. It is difficult to select a benchmark that can

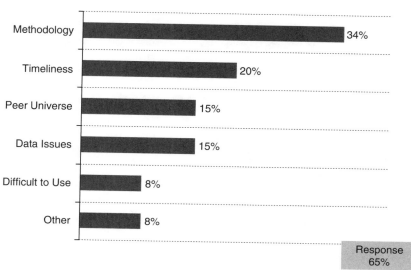

Exhibit 10.2 *Source:* TABB Group.

measure different kinds of transaction costs equally. Some benchmarks may not be appropriate for evaluating trades in stocks with widely different levels of liquidity and volatility. The primary benchmark that is used is the Volume-Weighted Average Price (VWAP). VWAP dominates as one of the most useful benchmarks because the concept is already well known and easy to understand. If, for example, an execution price is better than the average price (weighted by volume), then it is a good execution. Another popular benchmark is the arrival price for measuring absolute transaction costs.

There are currently a number of firms that provide post-trade TCR (see Exhibit 10.3). These providers include Plexus, Elkins-McSherry, and Abel-Noser, and other newcomers such as Quantative Services Group (QSG) and GTAnalytics. Firms such as QSG are focused on high-touch analyst outreach while NYFIX is focused on delivering real-time TCR. ITG has become a formidable challenger to other TCR providers through its purchase of Plexus.

10.3 Pre-Trade TCR

Pre-trade analytics offers historical and predictive data on price behavior or how a trade position might react to different trading strategies. It can help a buy-side trader justify an execution or help assess performance. The information can provide data on a single stock order or program

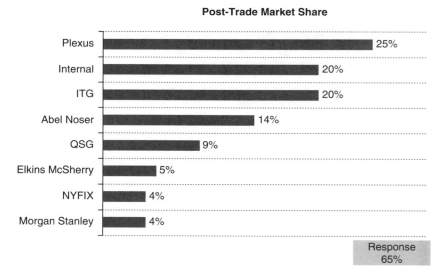

Post-Trade Market Share

Plexus	25%
Internal	20%
ITG	20%
Abel Noser	14%
QSG	9%
Elkins McSherry	5%
NYFIX	4%
Morgan Stanley	4%

Response 65%

Exhibit 10.3 *Source:* TABB Group.

trade details such as volume, volatility, illiquidity, and other risk characteristics (see Exhibit 10.4). For single stocks, a trader may analyze a number of
different parameters such as the share quantity or duration of the order.
Historical data or predictive modeling may derive estimates of the impact of
the order, or price movements. When the buy side executes illiquid stocks,
traders may have to analyze the risk of market impact and opportunity cost.
Electronic trades can be analyzed through risk characteristics, which include
the overall risk of the electronic trades the trader will pay to the various
brokers/dealers competing for the best bid. Pre-trade analytics are a critical
component of the bidding process on program trades, as traders often cite
the refusal of brokers to bid on a program without supporting cost validation.
Pre-trade data can enable the trader to identify whether the estimated costs
for a stock are attributable to volatility, spread, or lack of volume.

PRE-TRADE TRANSACTION COST RESEARCH PROVIDERS

Pre-trade analytics is an important aspect for vendors when providing
trading tools for the investment community. Brokers and vendors have a
variety of prepackaged products that may educate traders on a particular
stock and help avert high transaction costs before they happen. Pre-trade

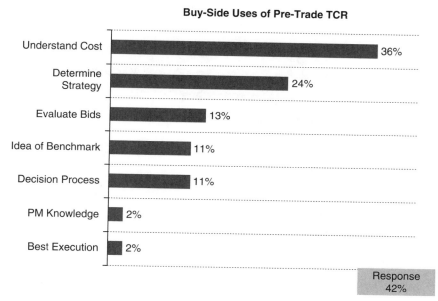

Buy-Side Uses of Pre-Trade TCR

Category	Percentage
Understand Cost	36%
Determine Strategy	24%
Evaluate Bids	13%
Idea of Benchmark	11%
Decision Process	11%
PM Knowledge	2%
Best Execution	2%

Response 42%

Exhibit 10.4   *Source:* TABB Group.

analytics is an important part of dialogue between traders and portfolio managers. One of the leading providers of TCR is ITG (see Exhibit 10.5). ITG was quick to integrate its pre-trade analytics and distribute the product efficiently to the investment community with first mover advantage. The inherent weaknesses of pre-trade analytics are accessibility and accuracy, along with the questionable willingness of investment firms to utilize it.

10.4 The Future of Transaction Cost Research

According to the TABB Group, TCR research products will continue to evolve based on four basic trends:

1. Integration into the trading platform
2. Customization of benchmarks
3. Flexible data formats
4. Pre-trade cost analytics

These basic trends will address the majority of issues investment firms face with transaction cost research. These include easy access, orders that must be judged based on multiple parameters, and the need to make better decisions at the time of order entry. Information being passed between trading platforms and TCR providers is a critical step between investment managers and broker-dealers. Execution platforms such as Portware and

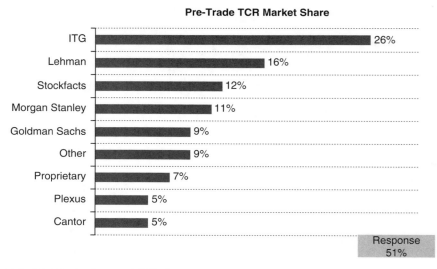

Exhibit 10.5 *Source:* TABB Group.

Flextrade have successfully integrated TCR into their trading engines. Direct market access platforms have the ability to calculate short-term transaction cost analysis in real-time utilizing trading information.

Pre-trade TCR may see radical improvements in the next few years. Most brokers currently offer two standard equity analytics: one for single stocks and another for baskets. Single-stock analytics may provide various attributes such as industry/sector, potential hedges, intraday volatility, and volume slices, which are simply average volume of stock over specified intraday intervals. Basket analytics can judge the overall risk in a basket, its exposure to different industries, and the potential implicit costs of the basket.

10.5 Conclusion

The interest in transaction cost research is widely attributable to increasing competition for lower transaction costs, and regulatory pressure. Investment managers are pushed to measure and manage transaction costs to increase investment returns, retain clients, attract new prospects, and satisfy regulators. When investment managers began to be judged by transaction costs, this began the push for algorithms and other advanced electronic execution tools. One universally known method of rating quality of execution is through achieving or exceeding the Volume-Weighted Average Price (VWAP). Broker-dealers have responded to the growing pressure from regulators and investment firms' desire for lowering transaction costs. Investment managers increasingly want to reduce implicit costs, and broker-dealers must fulfill this demand in order to retain client business. In the end, transaction cost research will be absorbed into the trading process, and soon incorporated into stock charts, annual reports, and employee compensation plans.

Chapter 11

Electronic and Algorithmic Trading for Different Asset Classes

11.1 Introduction

Web-based technologies have made substantial changes in the financial services industry. Virtual exchanges and extended after-market-hours trading have significantly accounted for transaction volume in stocks. The adoption of electronic trading platforms has transformed the economic landscape of trading, and other market-making possibilities. Current technologies such as algorithmic trading had been most often associated with one particular asset class: equities. Now algorithms, or mathematical models that take over the process of trading decisions and executions, are diversifying into other markets that are rapidly evolving toward electronic trading such as fixed-incomes, foreign exchange, derivatives, futures, and options. The move to systematic algorithmic approaches with derivatives may not seem as radical as it did in equities, because participants in these markets are comfortable with technology. Electronic access to stocks has been more prevalent than for futures and options, but these asset classes are catching up particularly in foreign exchange. The highly liquid but fragmented OTC foreign exchange market has very little to offer in terms of accepted execution benchmarks, making it difficult to measure algorithmic performance. One response to this problem is a rush to implement algorithmic trading tools based on technology borrowed from the equities markets. A growing number of trading platforms now support trading in OTC derivatives. According to the Bond Market Association in 2004, 25 platforms now allow users to execute transactions in interest rate swaps, credit default swaps, options, futures, and other derivative products, nearly double the number in 2003. The equities markets will execute trades using some sort of algorithmic model, but the same will most likely be true for other products such as futures, options, and foreign exchange. Fixed income will be one of the last to move along because it is predominantly a dealer market, but when it does, the first asset class will most likely be the most liquid sectors such as the U.S. Treasury market. The later arrival of electronic trading in fixed-income markets compared to equities reflects distinct differences between the two. Fixed-income products are far less homogenous, with many more separate and individually less liquid issues than equities. This makes it technically difficult and more expensive to introduce automated systems. There are millions of fixed-income instruments on issue in the U.S. alone (see Exhibit 11.1) with different coupon rates, maturities, varying frequency of interest payments, etc., compared to a few thousand listed shares. Most fixed-income venues have not opened up to pure Electronic Communication Networks (ECNs). Electronic trading has made the most inroads in government bond markets. Fixed-income trading is decidedly a different instrument, with numerous types of asset classes, and their complexities in comparison to simple common stock require a different use of technology and business design to compete in the evolving electronic landscape. Electronic trading in the U.S. and European markets has continued to develop and evolve, however, with trading platforms developing value-added services such as historical pricing data, confirmation, allocation services, order management systems, and electronic research delivery.

U.S. Fixed Income Market 2005

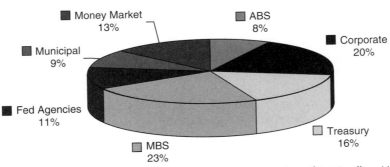

Exhibit 11.1 Breakdown of asset class and debt outstanding ($24.9 trillion USD). *Source:* Bond Market Association.

Electronic trading can widen access to trading systems across several dimensions. Physical limitations that once disabled access to traditional venues can now participate at marginal costs. This greater access has brought questions regarding the role of intermediaries. Shifts from pure dealer structures to continuous auction arrangements where users can transact directly with one another will continue to grow. This is already witnessed in large liquid markets, especially in equity and foreign exchange where investors can more easily match their requirements in a reasonable period of time. This wider access to trading systems increases pressure on dealers and typically forces investment banks to focus on more value-added services such as corporate finance, advisory services, and risk management.

A common benefit of electronic trading is greater trade transparency. Systems can disseminate real-time pre- and post-trade information. In today's markets, FIX protocols are used primarily to facilitate pre-trade and post-trade information. FIX, or Financial Information Exchange Protocol, is a technical specification for electronic communication of trade-related messages developed through the collaboration of banks, broker-dealers, exchanges, industry utilities, and associations. As the market's leading trade communications protocol, FIX is integral to order management and trading systems.

Electronic trading can also operate with minimum information leakage. The basic demand for anonymous trading can now be met through many platforms and systems. These transparencies tend to benefit one group of participants and their objectives while having negative effects on another. Transparency in electronic trading has become a regulatory focus because of greater choice of trading venues and routing options, and fairness of information access across the market. The demand for anonymous trading could magnify the possibility of a "liquidity sweep." This occurs when a buy-side trader requests firm offers or bids from several dealers at one time and instantaneously lifts all offers without disclosing the trader's intentions to any dealer. The trader is able to conceal the size of the firm's order, and the resulting purchases might be disruptive to the market as multiple dealers simultaneously attempt to liquidate their position. There is a strong possibility that dealers will not quote out their most competitive prices, thus reducing the efficiency of electronic trading platforms.

11.2 Development of Electronic Trading

Electronic trading has penetrated different sectors unevenly. Market structure, regulatory compliance, competitive factors, and the different asset classes have all proved to be deciding factors in the evolution of electronic trading. As new systems evolve, such as portfolio trading, with

Internet use being more widely integrated, the distinction between market sectors will begin to blur. The developments in equity, fixed-income, and foreign exchange markets are described below.

EQUITY MARKETS

Equity markets are the best known and most widely studied examples of electronic trading. Traditional markets in the United States such as telephone, over-the-counter, or floor- and specialist-traded securities are dominated by three national markets: the New York Stock Exchange, AMEX, and order-driven NASDAQ. Separate electronic trading systems have gained a foothold in the United States over recent decades. Currently, the NYSE said it would migrate to a hybrid market structure model increasing the use of real-time trade-matching technology and reduce their reliance on specialists to match highly liquid stocks. Transitioning to a hybrid electronic system will enable both buy-side and sell-side firms to route more order flow to the floor electronically, and highly liquid stocks can be matched electronically without the involvement of a specialist and floor broker. The move to a fully electronic market for liquid stocks will mean the elimination of specialists for those stocks, and they will only focus on large block orders. The exchange

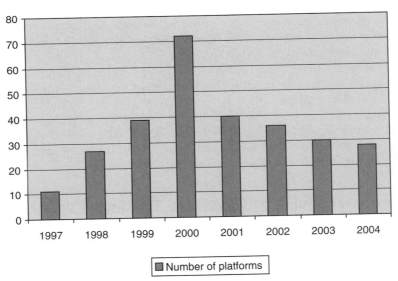

Number of Electronic Trading Platforms

Exhibit 11.2   *Source:* Aite Group estimates.

hopes to accomplish two things: to gain positive press, and to derail the push to repeal the trade-through rule, which is an attempt for ECNs to grab share away from the NYSE by allowing firms to execute orders away from the best price in the market. The two main criticisms of the NYSE have been its lack of speed and interference of specialists who are perceived as negative impact for market movement, leaving the market highly uncompetitive.

FIXED-INCOME MARKETS

The move to electronic trading in fixed-income markets has been slower than for equities. Algorithmic trading clearly suits the equity markets. Equity prices are transparent, there are fewer securities, and the availability of multiple execution channels allows savvy investors to exploit inefficiencies in the marketplace. For years, bonds of all types were typically traded in telephone dealer markets, where electronic systems have made limited inroads until recently. In the bond market, the interdealer broker (IDB) is the foundation in which most algorithmic trading is played out. Brokers such as eSpeed and BrokerTec trade one of the more actively traded markets for U.S. Treasury bonds, which provide enough liquidity needed for algorithmic trading to be effective. More thinly traded sectors such as credit markets don't offer consistent enough pricing to effectively utilize an algorithmic trading model.[1] The late arrival of electronic trading in fixed-income markets compared to equities reflects distinct differences between the two. By 2008, electronic trading will account for over 60% of total U.S. fixed-income trading volume (see Exhibits 11.2 and 11.3), as leading platforms continue to expand into less liquid products, according to the Aite Group. Competition is expanding into less liquid Fixed-income instruments, which include European markets, algorithmic trading, and OTC derivative products such as interest rate swaps and credit derivatives. The marketplace has also witnessed contraction in the number of trading platforms from its peak in 2000, when over 70 electronic fixed-income trading platforms existed, to fewer than 30 platforms remaining at the end of 2004. Realistically, only a handful of those remaining platforms can be considered legitimate.

The U.S. fixed-income market has evolved substantially since the late 1990s when most electronic trading took place on interdealer markets. At the end of 1998, approximately 2.6% of fixed-income trading was conducted electronically according to estimates projected by the Aite Group. By the end of 2004, that figure jumped to over 35%. The Aite Group expects the rate to reach over 60% by the end of 2008.

---

[1] Billy Hult, "Algorithmic Trading in the Bond Markets," *Electronic Trading Outlook, Wall Street Letter*, June 2006: 15–16, http://www.rblt.com/documents/hybridsupplement.pdf.

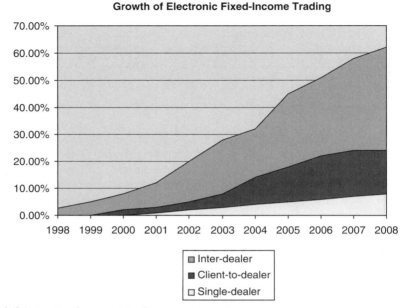

Exhibit 11.3 *Source:* Aite Group estimates.

U.S. Treasury products dominate trading volume with approximately US $500 billion traded daily, followed by mortgage-backed securities with US $205 billion (see Exhibit 11.4). The last four years have seen an increase in less liquid fixed-income issues such as corporate bonds.

11.3 Electronic Trading Platforms

Leading fixed-income dealers have operated their own proprietary platforms for many years. Large clients can access their inventory directly. The advantage of a proprietary platform is its ability to provide research, advanced analytics, and electronic access to different asset classes. These platforms can also be linked with multidealer platforms, and other market terminals such as Bloomberg, Reuters, and Thomson Financial. Multidealer platforms such as TradeWeb, MarketAxess, BondVision, and the Muni-Center have done a tremendous job of increasing market transparency providing STP solutions, and increasing secondary trading activities in their respective markets (see Exhibit 11.5). During the last several years, interdealer platforms have been on the rise with eSpeed and ICAP engaging

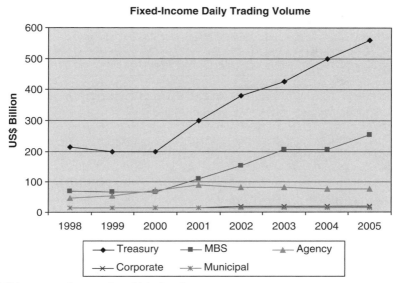

Exhibit 11.4   *Source:* Bond Market Association.

in intense competition. The global interdealer market has contracted in the last few years as a result of consolidation.

Currently, most electronic trading activities have taken place in U.S. Treasuries. Approximately 68% of U.S. Treasuries were electronically executed by the end of 2004 according to the Aite Group. The MBS market was a distant second with 30% penetration, and the U.S. corporate bond

Firm	Headquarters	Type of Platform	Number of Clients	Average Daily Volume
Bond Desk	Mill Valley, CA	Retail Focus multi-dealer	80 broker dealers; In excess of 2,000 firms and corresponding clearing networks	16,000 trades per day
eSpeed	New York, NY	Inter-dealer	~700	US $200 billion
ICAP	London, UK	Inter-dealer	>250	US $400 billion
MarketAxess	New York, NY	Multi-dealer	500 buy side 22 sell side	US $1.45 billion
TheMuniCenter	New York, NY	Multi-dealer	650	N/A
Thomson **TradeWeb**	Jersey City, NJ	Multi-dealer	1,800 buy side 34 dealers,160 sell-side trading desks globally	US $1.48 billion

Exhibit 11.5   Background of different trading platforms. *Source:* Aite Group.

Firm	U.S. Treasuries	MBS	Agency	Corporate Bonds	Munis	European Issues	Derivatives
Bond Desk	x		x	x	x		
eSpeed	x		x			x	x
ICAP	x	x	x			x	x
MarketAxess				x		x	
TheMuniCenter	x			x	x		
TradeWeb	x	x	x	x		x	x

Exhibit 11.6 Products supported. *Source:* Aite Group.

market currently stands at 9% with growth potential with ECNs such as MarketAxess and Thomson's TradeWeb competing for additional market share (see Exhibit 11.6). Currently, the focus on client-to-dealer market trading has turned to credit markets as Thomson's TradeWeb forces its way into corporate bond markets to compete directly with MarketAxess. TradeWeb is the current market leader in liquid fixed-income products such as treasuries, but MarketAxess is the dominant player in illiquid markets. Fixed-income platforms are also moving into derivatives with most of the attention focused on interest rate swaps and credit derivatives (see Exhibit 11.7). Other trading venues such as algorithmic trading are still immature in market penetration for fixed-income instruments, with a growing number of firms looking to gain access to historical transaction data for analysis. Liquid fixed-income markets should benefit greatly from this opportunity.

U.S. corporate debt and their derivatives have become one of the fastest-growing segments of the U.S. fixed-income market. By 2006, the total notional outstanding credit derivatives market is expected to reach US $8.5–9.0 trillion. One of the most interesting developments in E-bond trading over the past 18 months has occurred in credit markets. Market-Axess, the unquestioned market leader in high-grade corporate debt, recently rolled out the first multi-dealer-to-client trading platform for credit

Firms	Products	Launch Date	Market Focus
eSpeed	Interest Rate Swaps	2003	Europe and U.S.
ICAP	Interest Rate Swaps	Q3 2004	Europe
	Credit Derivatives	Q4 2004	Europe and U.S.
MarketAxess	Credit Derivatives	Q3 2005	Europe and U.S.
Thomson TradeWeb	Interest Rate Swaps	Q1 2005 for Euro Q3 2005 for U.S.	Europe and U.S.
	Credit Derivatives	Q3 2005 for U.S.	Europe and U.S.

Exhibit 11.7 Expansion into derivatives. *Source:* Firms.

default swaps. MarketAxess is now facing increased competition from Thomson TradeWeb. U.S. corporate debt outstanding currently stands at US \$5.0 trillion, accounting for 20% of all U.S. fixed-income securities outstanding by notional amount. Corporates, however, remain one of the most illiquid segments of the U.S. bond market with trading volume as of Q2 2005 at just US \$20.9 billion average trading volume per day representing over 2% of all fixed-income activity. Corporates have long suffered from a lack of transparency. Information was based solely on conversations with brokers or dealers. Buy-side investors had to call dealers to get liquidity and pricing information, which was often incomplete or conflicting.[2]

11.4 Types of Systems

- **Auction systems**   These enable participants to conduct electronic auctions of securities offerings. Some auction systems are tailored to new issues in the primary market. Others focus on auctions of secondary market offerings by investors or others. In either case, a seller or issuer typically posts the details of a security being offered for sale and the specific terms of the auction, whether the auction is single price or multiple price, the time the auction is open, whether partial orders will be filled, etc. Buyers are able to submit bids for the offered securities, and the offering is awarded to the bidder that offers the highest price or lowest yield. In some cases, the identities of the bidders and the amounts of the bids are kept anonymous.
- **Cross-matching systems**   These generally bring both dealers and institutional investors together in electronic trading networks that provide real-time or periodic cross-matching sessions. Customers are able to enter anonymous buy and sell orders with multiple counterparties that are automatically executed when contra-side orders are entered at the same price when the posted prices are "hit" or "lifted." In some cases, customers are able to initiate negotiation sessions to establish the terms of trades.
- **Interdealer systems**   These allow dealers to execute transactions electronically with other dealers through the fully anonymous services of interdealer brokers.
- **Multidealer systems**   These provide customers with consolidated orders from two or more dealers and provide customers with the ability to execute from among multiple quotes. Often, multidealer systems

(continues)

---

[2] Harrell Smith, "Fixed Income Trading 2005: Electronic Credit Markets and TRACE Take Center Stage," *Building an Edge* 6 no. 10 (November 15, 2005): 1–3.

Continued

display to customers the best bid or ask price for a given security among all the prices posted by participating dealers. These systems also generally allow investors to request quotes for a particular security or type of security from one or more dealers. Participating dealers generally act as principals in transitions. A variety of security types are offered through these systems.

- **Single-dealer systems**   These allow investors to execute transactions directly with a specific dealer of choice, with the dealer acting as principal in each transaction. Dealers offer access through a combination of third-party providers, proprietary networks, and the Internet.[3]

11.5 TRACE—Reform in Transparency

On January 23, 2001, the Securities and Exchange Commission (SEC) approved the first major transparency initiative in the OTC secondary corporate bond markets. The National Association of Securities Dealers (NASD) launched the first phase of a three-part initiative that all dealers and interdealers report the prices of corporate bond trades to its Trade Reporting and Compliance Engine (TRACE). At the time of its launch, U.S. broker-dealers were required to provide NASD transaction information on bonds sold or bought within a 75-minute time frame. Beginning in July 2002, the NASD publicly disseminated that information in near-real time for 500 eligible investment-grade corporate bonds and for 50 high-yield bonds. Phase 2 of the TRACE rollout began in March 2003 when the NASD publicly disseminated single-A and better bonds with an initial issuance size of $100 million. By February 2005, TRACE reporting was reduced to a 30-minute period and most U.S. dollar–denominated corporate bond trades became eligible for public dissemination. New-issue BBB and below bonds and bonds that average less than one transaction per day and are rated BB in a transaction worth over $1 million are allowed dissemination delays. In the final step, which occurred in July of 2006, TRACE reportable bonds were reduced to 15 minutes from the time of trade to time of being reported. The presumption is that the NASD will eliminate any remaining delays in the near future. The new price information available will allow third-party vendors and financial Web sites to provide valuable and easy-to-navigate services for disseminating TRACE data. These vendors include Bloomberg,

---

[3] The Bond Market Association, "eCommerce in the Fixed-Income Markets: The 2003 Review of Electronic Transaction Systems," http://www.bondmarkets.com/assets/files/ets_report_1103.pdf.

BondDeskGroup, General Associates, MarketAxess, Reuters, Telekurs Financial, and TradeWeb, among others.[4]

THE RESULTS OF REGULATORY REFORM

The expected benefits of increased price transparency include:

1. an increase in market efficiency;
2. new market participants;
3. better risk and portfolio management;
4. the enabling of sophisticated trading strategies;
5. a decrease in improper trade practices;
6. better valuation models;
7. enhanced technology.

Even if the desired impact of price transparency occurs through the tightening of bid/offer spreads, saving corporate bond investors money, some market participants believe the measurable impact is small. As competition in U.S. corporate fixed-income markets become fiercer and a whole new generation of retail investors purchase corporate bonds, the SEC will implement further regulatory action such as greater oversight of credit rating agencies.[5] Sell-side corporate traders lost $1 billion in commissions a year after regulators required securities prices to be publicly disclosed, according to the *Journal of Financial Economics*. The difference between bid-ask spread for corporate bonds narrowed by 8 basis points in the first year after TRACE was introduced in July 2002. The real benefactor of TRACE reporting has been the buy side, especially institutional investors who trade in smaller lots. Smaller firms gained market share and broker-dealers lost revenue, as all traders were able to share the same prices. The transparency created by TRACE has squeezed soft dollar revenue for the sell side, causing broker-dealers to cut back on bond-research departments. At the same time, income is booming from securities that are derived from corporate bonds. The market for credit default swaps has more than doubled in size in the past year to cover $26 trillion of securities, according to the International Swaps and Derivatives Association (ISDA). Swaps allow traders to bet on creditworthiness of companies without actually owning the underlying bonds. In March 2006, the NYSE began seeking approval to start electronic trading of 4,000 corporate bonds.

---

[4] Harrell Smith, "Fixed Income Trading 2005: Electronic Credit Markets and TRACE Take Center Stage," *Building an Edge* 6 no. 10 (November 15, 2005): 7–9.

[5] Ibid.: 10.

11.6 Foreign Exchange Markets

Electronic trading has had an important presence in inter-dealer spot foreign exchange market for over a decade. The Bank of International Settlements shows that 20–30% of interbank trading in major currencies was executed electronically in 1995, rising to 50% in 1998 and estimated at over 90% by 2001. For years, there have been two major systems, EBS and Reuters. Both systems have been designed as order books, in which dealers can see the best bid and offer in the market, alongside the best bid and offer that could be traded. Electronic systems are now used for the majority of spot inter-dealer trading in major currencies. While the structure of the foreign exchange market was a fragmented telephone market before the introduction of electronic trading, many of the leading ECNs in foreign exchange were designed for humans using keypads entering orders. These systems were designed in the late 70s and early 80s when achieving electronic execution in one second was considered a vast improvement over the telephone. One of the consistent results in the evolution from voice to electronic trading is more tickets and smaller amounts when transactions became more efficient. These ECNs have grown with this natural increase in volume, but managing that growth from a technology perspective has proved challenging given their legacy system environments. One strategy employed by ECNs with legacy technology is order throttling (limiting the number of orders that a connection can submit into the market). As a result, active participants may be rejected when they attempt to hit a price even though the price is available and the data feed is accurate. New entrants such as CME and Currenex have begun to exploit these weaknesses and gain market share because of the reduced latency they can offer.

Most foreign exchange algorithmic execution models were developed for the buy-side equities market. They leverage the anonymity the central counterparty brings to the table to hide patterns, which would create market impact in a non-anonymous OTC market. When these models are used to trade foreign exchange on direct bank relationships, they rapidly lose their desired effect and can have negative impact on execution performance. Most algorithmic execution models (order slicing for example) require 100% anonymous trading on a central counterparty model to protect the identity of the trader at all times. Additionally, ECNs must not provide market makers with customer identifiers (as many FX ECNs do), which give market makers the ability to reverse engineer individual models.

Credit and anonymity will continue to have a strong effect on foreign exchange markets. While algorithmic execution models play an important role in equities, there are also many other execution models that have flourished. In particular, call-auction block trading systems which allow funds to trade large sizes with little or no market impact and total anonymity play an important role in equities but do not exist yet in foreign exchange.

Hedge funds are positioned as the obvious innovators in leveraging proprietary execution models to trade large volumes across multiple liquidity pools. Taking a more conservative approach are the real-money funds and corporations who, using standard execution models focused on certainty of execution (RFQ) and benchmark trading procedures, may find algorithmic trading platforms an inefficient alternative to traditional trading models. Finally, the sell-side is beginning to use algorithmic models on their trading desks, enhancing their own strategies to manage risks and employing their own automated strategies to keep pace with the booming foreign exchange industry. Banks will probably have the most to gain from this new technology, as well as the most to lose if they fail to adapt.[6]

11.7 The FX Market Ecosystem

Algorithms are beginning to surface in the foreign exchange markets. The opportunities for fast and effective electronic trading in the FX markets have resulted in over US $2 trillion in trades each day. Of this, 48% is spot markets. Among the major currencies, EUR/USD represents 26%, USD/GBP represents 15% and USD/JPY represents 12% of the spot markets.

According to Currenex, 80% of the volume for these pairs is traded between 7:00 and 17:00 GMT. Therefore, peak hours of liquidity is approximately $11M per second for EUR/USD, $6.4M per second for GBP/USD, and $5.1M per second for USD/JPY. These are only average volumes at peak hours and do not account for bursts of trading activity and do not take into account price volatility. The spot FX market is comprised of a variety of participants, including: banks, hedge funds, investment managers, corporations, and speculators. Together these participants create an ecosystem of liquidity. When large trades enter this ecosystem, short-term price volatility occurs. However, over time, the trade is absorbed into the ecosystem and price stability returns. Any participant planning to execute large orders must understand the rate at which liquidity can be absorbed with nominal price impact.[7]

Buy-side and sell-side participants continue to advance their sophistication in the FX marketplace. New technologies are crucial in assuring faster, better fills at the time an algorithmic model executes an order. Mechanisms

---

[6] Sean Gilman, "Demistifying Algorithmic Trading," *Currenex*, June, 2006.
[7] Sean Gilman, "Algorithmic Trading and its Effect on the FX Ecosystem," *FX Trading Solutions, Currenex*, 2007.

that route orders between disparate market venues based on customer criteria play an important role. Automated trading is about timing and execution, so every millisecond counts; therefore, if an order match exists, then a match must occur across liquidity pools with minimal slippage. As more users use smart order routing technologies, this becomes a game of splitting milliseconds with computer models competing with each other for access to limited liquidity. This makes technologies that allow a single order to exist in multiple markets simultaneously critical for algorithmic execution models. Scalable connectivity for placing trades quickly and efficiently with full integration of information among all participants is another key ally as these new technologies promise to better route orders in multiple liquidity pools to execute in asymmetric relationships. At the end of an algorithm's cycle, the trade is only as good as the order routing technology existing on the platform where it has been employed.

11.8 Conclusion

Algorithmic trading clearly suits the equity and foreign exchange markets for the time being. There are fewer instruments, prices are transparent, liquidity is concentrated, and the availability of multiple execution channels allows savvy investors to exploit inefficiencies. The bond market, however, is dominated by a handful of large brokers such as eSpeed and BrokerTec, most of which is centered on actively traded markets such as U.S. Treasury bonds, the only current fixed-income market that is able to provide the liquidity needed for algorithmic trading to be effective. Thinly traded sectors such as credit markets don't offer consistent pricing in sufficient size to fit an algorithmic trading model. The implementation of TRACE reporting, however, is beginning to bridge that gap and provide more transparency in credit markets. Most traditional investment managers trade electronically by submitting a request for quote (RFQ) through an ECN to dealers. The growth of algorithmic trading is contingent on the growth of trading multi-assets globally. As the barriers between markets fall, technology becomes more sophisticated, and the marketplace begins to offer trading on a single platform in all asset classes, there is opportunity for real-time cross-asset pricing. The growth of algorithmic trading will be linked to how quickly the barriers between markets fall as trading across asset classes becomes more prominent globally.

Chapter 12

Regulation NMS and Other Regulatory Reporting

12.1 Introduction

On April 26, 2005, the Securities and Exchange Commission (SEC) approved the Regulation National Market System ("Reg NMS"). The implementation of Reg NMS is designed to modernize and strengthen the more than 5,000 listed companies within the NMS. At the time this book was written, the projected deadline in which Reg NMS–compliant trading systems must be operational was February 7, 2007. The pilot stocks phase will begin May 21, 2007. This represents $14 trillion in market capitalization trading on nine different market centers. The SEC strengthened the NMS to update antiquated rules and promote equal regulation of different types of stocks and markets while displaying greater liquidity. Regulation NMS includes two amendments designed to disseminate market information, and includes new rules designed to modernize and strengthen the regulatory structure of U.S. equity markets:

- Order Protection Rule or new Trade-Through Rule
- Access Rule
- Sub-Penny Pricing
- Market Data Rules and Plans

Reg NMS was developed to clarify controversies between executing through slow inefficient markets and faster expedient ones. The Trade-

Through Rule currently exists under listed exchanges but exempts NAS-DAQ markets. The new mandate will specify that an exchange cannot execute an order at a worse price if a better price is available. This will potentially eliminate the entire floor-based exchange model. The second aspect of Reg NMS is the Access Rule, which opens up the Inter-market Trading System (ITS) connecting exchanges to private competition. The Access Rule caps exchanges and ECNs from charging more than $.003 per share. The Sub-Penny Pricing Rule prohibits participants (ECNs, exchanges, market makers, and alternative trading systems) from displaying or accepting quotes in NMS stock that are priced in increments of less than a penny unless the stock is already priced under $1.00. The rule prevents hedge funds and other active traders from gaining execution priority by improving price of a limit order through insignificant amounts. Market Data Rules are designed to promote the wide availability of market data and to allocate revenues to self-regulatory organizations (SROs) that produce the most useful data for investors. It strengthens the existing market data system, which provides investors in the U.S. equity markets with real-time access to the best quotations and most recent trades in the thousands of NMS stocks throughout the trading day. Investors of all types have access to a reliable source of information for the best prices in NMS stocks.

12.2 Regulatory Challenges

The increase in technology and the Internet have had a profound effect on the structure of equity markets. The list of regulatory challenges can be an overwhelming task as investors will be able with just a click to trade their way away from any market that can hide questionable and possibly illegal activities from U.S. market surveillance. The issues that confront the Securities and Exchange Commission (SEC) and the U.S. equity markets are highly complex, and while the SEC has not set a timetable to resolve these issues, a speedy resolution is imperative for the survival of many markets. The list of challenges for regulators can include oversight of a global settlement system, the prevention of fraud, the enforcement of stock-holder and investor rights, the collection of fees and taxes, and the integration of laws that constantly require updating. In recent years, both the NYSE and NASDAQ have significantly updated their governance and self-regulatory structures. The NYSE has created a new, independent board and established an autonomous regulatory unit that reports directly to a fully independent regulatory oversight committee of the board. These changes are designed to significantly improve the governance and regulatory functions of the NYSE.

Most U.S. stocks are listed in the nation's two primary markets, the New York Stock Exchange (NYSE) and the NASDAQ Stock Market (NASDAQ). Investors have a variety of options where they may trade these securities. Some are electronic and others still depend on human interaction. Investors can now evaluate the quality of their executions through other market centers. These scenarios were made possible by regulatory intervention designed to promote competition and innovation. The SEC has intervened repeatedly to allow newer trading systems to compete with more traditional markets, to strike down rules that favor one set of participants over another, and to make investors more aware of what goes on behind closed doors at other investment houses. Under the SEC's oversight, self-regulatory organizations (SROs) regulate trading in U.S. equities. The NYSE and NASD and other regional stock exchanges have set out to enforce rules that regulate their own members.

As of 2005, the NYSE executes approximately 78% of share volume in NYSE stocks, most of which is executed manually. The NYSE has recognized that new regulation NMS has transformed competition between equity trades, protecting only automated quotations that are immediately accessible. Management of the NYSE has worked steadily to develop its own Hybrid Market proposal, which is designed to give investors a choice of executing orders automatically or sending them to the floor for manual execution. Two major competitors of the NYSE's Hybrid Market are likely to be the new NASDAQ, which currently reports 15% of share volume in NYSE stocks, and the Archipelago Exchange, which is a fully electronic market that currently reports 2% of volume in NYSE stocks. The hybrid and electronic markets were designed to create greater automated trading and substantial benefits for investors in faster, more efficient trading particularly in NYSE stocks. Regional exchanges and other types of market centers are now becoming an increasing threat competing for market share in NYSE stocks. These include automated matching systems that seek to facilitate the large trades of institutional investors with anonymity and without telegraphing their trading interests to broader markets.

12.3　The National Market System[1]

The United States is fortunate to have equity markets characterized by extremely vigorous competition among a variety of different types of markets. There are five types of markets.

---

[1] Securities and Exchange Commission, *Regulation NMS* www.sec.gov/rules/proposed/34-49325.htm.

1. Traditional exchanges with active trading floors, which even now are evolving to expand the range of choices that they offer investors for both automated and manual trading.
2. Purely electronic markets, which offer both standard limit orders and conditional orders that are designated to facilitate complex trading strategies.
3. Market-making securities dealers, which offer both automated execution of smaller orders and the commitment of capital to facilitate the automated systems for executing of smaller orders and the commitment of capital to facilitate the execution of larger, institutional orders.
4. Regional exchanges, many of which have adopted automated systems for executing smaller orders.
5. Automated matching systems that permit investors, particularly large institutions, to seek counter-parties to their trades anonymously and with minimal market impact.[2]

The Securities and Exchange Commission adopted the National Market System (NMS), which was implemented to serve two main functions. It was designed to facilitate trading of OTC stocks whose size, profitability, and trading activity meet specific criteria, and it was designed to post prices for securities on the NYSE and other regional exchanges simultaneously, allowing investors to obtain the best prices. In recent years, the equity markets have experienced sweeping changes, ranging from new technologies to new types of markets to the initiation of trading in penny increments. During the last five years, the SEC has undertaken a broad and systematic review to determine how best to keep the NMS up to date. Congress has placed great emphasis in catering to long-term investors since 84 million individuals representing more than half of American households own equity securities. Seventy million of these individuals participate indirectly in equity markets through ownership of mutual fund shares. Regulation NMS includes two amendments designed to disseminate market information, and new rules designed to modernize and strengthen the regulatory structure of U.S. equity markets.

1. A new Order Protection Rule, which reinforces the fundamental principle of obtaining the best price for investors when such price is represented by automated quotations that are immediately accessible.
2. A new Access Rule, which promotes fair and nondiscriminatory access to quotations displayed by the NMS trading centers through a private linkage approach.

---

[2] U.S. Senate Committee on Banking, Housing, and Urban Affairs, William H. Donaldson, *Testimony Concerning Recent Developments in the Equity Markets*, May 19, 2005, http://www.sec.gov/news/testimony/ts051905whd.htm.

3. A new Sub-Penny Pricing Rule, which establishes a uniform quoting increment of no less than one penny for quotation in NMS stocks equal to or greater than $1.00 per share to promote price transparency and consistency.
4. Amendments to the Market Date Rules and joint industry plans that allocate plan revenues to self-regulatory organizations (SRO) for their contributions to public price discovery and promote wider and more efficient distribution of market data.
5. A reorganization of the existing Exchange Act governing the NMS to promote clarity and understanding of the rules.

Prior to Regulation NMS, the lack of consistent intermarket trading rules for NMS stocks had divided the equity markets into a market for exchange-listed stocks and a market for NASDAQ stocks; these stocks traded in different regulatory structures. Exchange-listed stocks were subject to the Intermarket Trading System (ITS) rules. These rules include trade-through restrictions, restrictions on locking or crossing quotations, and participation in a "hard" linage system. The result of the ITS rules has been a less than optimal regulatory environment for both exchange-listed and NASDAQ stocks. The ITS trade provisions were from an era of manual markets.

The NMS encompasses the stocks of more than 5,000 listed companies, which collectively represent more than $14 trillion in U.S. market capitalization. These stocks are traded simultaneously at a variety of different venues that participate in the NMS, including national securities exchanges, alternative trading systems (ATS), and market-making securities dealers. The NMS approach is widely believed to be the primary reason that U.S. equity markets are widely recognized as being the fairest, most efficient, and most competitive in the world. Through constant modernization, the NMS rules are designed to ensure that the equity markets will continue to serve the interests of investors, listed companies, and the public.

The NMS was created to promote fair competition among individual markets, while ensuring that all of these markets are linked together in a unified system that promotes interaction among the orders of buyers and sellers in a particular NMS stock. Aggressive competition among markets promotes more efficient and innovative trading services, while integrated competition among orders promotes more efficient pricing of individual stocks for all types of orders, large and small. Together, they produce markets that offer the greatest benefits for investors and listed companies. Foreign markets with significant equity trading typically have a single, overwhelmingly dominant public market. The United States, however, is fortunate to have equity markets that are characterized by vigorous competition among a variety of different markets. Some of these include traditional exchanges with active trading floors offering investors with automated and manual trading; purely electronic markets that offer both standard limit orders and conditional orders that are designed to facilitate complex trading strategies; market-making securities dealers, which offer both automated execution of smaller orders and commitment of capital to facilitate the execution of large orders; and regional exchanges that have adopted auto-mated systems for executing smaller orders and the automated matching systems that permit investors to seek counterparties to trade anonymously with minimal price impact.

The SEC has been reviewing market structure issues and assessing how best to achieve an appropriate balance between competition among markets and competition among orders, and they concluded that one of the most impor-tant goals of equity markets is to minimize transaction costs for long-term investors in order to reduce the cost of capital for listed companies. Most of the time, the interests of short-term traders and long-term investors will not conflict. Short-term traders clearly provide valuable liquidity to the market. When the interests of long-term investors and short-term traders diverge, forming public policy for the U.S. equity markets becomes fundamentally important. The objective of minimizing short-term price volatility offers an important example where the interests of long-term investors can diverge from those of short-term traders. Liquid markets that minimize volatility are usually the most beneficial to long-term investors. Such markets help reduce transaction costs by furthering the ability of investors to establish and unwind positions in a stock without moving bid and ask spreads. Exces-sively volatile markets can generate many opportunities for traders to earn short-term profits from rapid price swings. Short-term traders, in particular, typically possess the capabilities and expertise necessary to enter and exit the market rapidly, exploiting such price swings. Short-term traders also have flexibility in establishing a long or short position, and the time of entering and exiting the market. Institutional and retail investors tend to invest for the long haul and typically have an opinion on the long-term prospects for a company. These investors are inherently less able to exploit short-term price swings, and their buying and selling interest often can initiate short-term price move-ments. Efficient markets with maximum liquidity and depth minimize such price movements and thereby afford long-term investors an opportunity to achieve their trading objectives with the lowest possible transaction costs. The SEC and NMS have focused their interests for long-term retail and institu-tional investors who depend on the performance of their equity investments, which are vital for retirement security and education. Investment returns can be reduced by high transaction costs including explicit costs of commissions and mutual fund fees. A largely hidden cost, however, is associated with prices of explicit costs of trading.

The strength of the NMS is critically dependent on the effectiveness of the SROs as regulators. There is clearly room for improvement in industry self-regulation. A series of proposals have been implemented to strengthen industry self-regulation. These include potential conflicts of interest between an SRO's regulatory obligations and the interests of its members, the potential costs and inefficiencies of multiple SRO models, the challenges of surveillance across markets by multiple SROs, and the manner in which SROs generate revenue and fund regulatory operations. Two of the major concerns include the NYSE becoming a publicly held company, and the proposed consolidation of the Instinet trading platform incorporated into NASDAQ. The NYSE would raise potential conflicts of interests between the interests of its shareholders and the need for effective self regulation. The NYSE would have to implement a truly autonomous regulatory staff. The consolidation of the Instinet platform incorporated into Nasdaq would result in two regulatory entities—the NASD and NASDAQ.

12.4 The Impact of Regulatory NMS

The number of brokers employed by the buy side will decrease as volume of market data flow increases significantly. The effects of NMS will escalate competition between brokers, and sell-side firms will need to identify the best execution that increases the importance of smart order routing to ensure the best execution. Broker-dealers will need considerably greater capacity to support the radical growth of market data. As more order flow moves electronically, there can be as much as a ten times multiplier in the amount of market data generated as sophisticated algorithms cancel and replace orders looking for liquidity, according to the TABB Group.

An increase in volume for both cancellations and quotes has been witnessed in the industry because each order typically creates a quote and each cancellation produces a revision to that quote. As message rates increase, both quote feeds are impacted. The TABB Group estimates that since 2000, the combined number of cancellations and quotes per trade on major exchanges has expanded more than 25 times. Regulation NMS has placed greater importance on routing, driving the accelerated use of black boxes and other electronic execution vehicles. The TABB Group expects that by the end of 2007 the messages per trade will approach 200.

NMS RULES IN DEPTH

The Trade-Through Rule or Order Protection Rule was designed to provide protection against a trade-through for all NMS stocks. A trade-through is defined as executing an order at a price that is inferior to the price of a guaranteed or protected quotation, which can often be a limit order displayed by another trading center. An order protection rule is designed to enhance protection of displayed prices, encourage greater use of limit orders, and contribute to increased market liquidity and depth. It is also designed to promote more fair and vigorous competition among orders seeking to supply liquidity. The Trade-Through Rule only protects quotations that are accessible through an automated execution system. It was designed to address the weakness set by the Intermarket Trading System (ITS). The ITS provision was implemented for floor-based markets and fails to reflect the difference in response time for manual and automated quotations. The ITS trade provisions require order routers to wait for responses from a manual market such as the floor of an exchange. The Trade-Through Rule bypasses this inefficiency and promotes fair competitions, eliminating priority given to these manual markets. The SEC believes that intermarket price protection benefits investors and strengthens the NMS for both exchange-listed securities and NASDAQ stocks.

Trading stocks involves three primary functions. The first function is the gathering of trading orders. The second function is the execution of these orders. The third function is the settlement of these trades. These functions usually reside in different organizations within an institution such as front, middle, and back office.

The Access Rule sets forth new standards governing access to quotations in NMS stocks. First, it enables the use of private linkages offered by a variety of connectivity providers. The lower cost and increased flexibility of connectivity in recent years has made private linkages a feasible alternative to hard linkages. Market participants may obtain indirect access to quotations displayed by a particular trading center through the members, subscribers, or customers of that trading center. Second, the rule generally limits the fees that any trading center can charge for accessing its protected quotations to no more than $.003 per share. The purpose of the fee limitation is to ensure the fairness and accuracy of displayed quotations by establishing an outer limit on the cost of accessing such quotations. The SEC believes that a single, uniform fee limitation of $.003 per share is the fairest and most appropriate resolution of the access fee issue. It will not interfere with current business practices, as trading centers have very few fees on their books of more than $.003 per share or earn substantial revenues from such fees. The fee limitation is necessary to support the integrity of the price protection requirement established by the adopted Order Protection Rule.

The Sub-Penny Pricing Rule prohibits market participants from displaying, ranking, or accepting quotations in NMS stocks that are priced in an increment of less than $0.01, unless the price of the quotation is less than $1.00. If the price of the quotation is less than $1.00, the minimum increment is $0.0001. The sub-penny proposal is a means to promote greater price transparency and consistency in displayed limit orders.

Market Data Rules are designed to promote the wide availability of market data and to allocate revenues to SROs that produce the most useful data for investors. They strengthen the existing market data system, which provides investors in the U.S. equity markets with real-time access to the best quotations and most recent trades in the thousands of NMS stocks throughout the trading day. Investors of all types have access to reliable sources of information for the best prices in NMS stocks.

12.5 Markets in Financial Instruments Directive in Europe

The Markets in Financial Instruments Directive (MiFID) came into effect in April 2004 and will apply to European investment firms and regulated markets by late 2007. The goal of MiFID is to increase the transparency and accessibility of markets to ensure price formation and protect investors. Like Reg NMS, it achieves this goal through regulating market transparency, order-routing requirements, and best execution (see Table 12.1). The MiFID will introduce a single market and regulatory regime and be applicable to 25 member states of the European Union.

The key aspects of MiFID[3] are as follows:

- **Authorization, regulation, and passporting** Firms covered by the MiFID will be authorized and regulated in their home state or registered office. Once a firm is authorized, it will be able to use the MiFID passport to provide services to customers in other EU member states.
- **Client classification** MiFID requires firms to classify clients as eligible counterparties, professional clients, and retail clients. Clear procedures must be in place to classify clients and assess their suitability for each type of investment product.
- **Client order handling** MiFID has requirements relating to the information that needs to be captured when accepting client orders, ensuring that a firm is acting in a client's best interests and as to how orders for different clients may be aggregated.

(continues)

---

[3] Wikipedia contributors, s.v. "Markets in Financial Instruments Directive (MiFID)," *Wikipedia, The Free Encyclopedia*, http://en.wikipedia.org/wiki/MiFID.

Table 12.1   Comparison Between Reg NMS and MiFID

	Reg NMS	MiFID
Current regulatory framework	ITS Plan Securities Exchange Act	Investment Services Directive and its implementation in the national laws of the EU member states
Regulatory authority	SEC	EU Commission and competent authorities of EU member states
To be applied from	To be determined	Tentatively Nov 2007
Trading venue classifications	Fast markets Slow markets	Regulated markets MTRs Systematic Internalizers
Best execution approach	NBBO as defined benchmark	Best results based on a multitude of parameters Best Execution Policy to be defined individually by Investment Firms
Objectives	Modernize and strengthen the NMS Reflect changes, ranging from new technologies to new types of markets and to structural changes	Establish a regulatory framework to promote an efficient, transparent, and integrated financial trading infrastructure Strengthen provisions governing investment services, with a view to protecting investors and fostering market integrity Extend the scope of the ISD, in terms of both financial services and financial instruments covered Reinforce cooperation between competent authorities

Source: Peter Gomber and Markus Gsell, *Catching Up with Technology: The Impact of Regulatory Changes on ECNs/MTFs.*

Continued

- **Pre-trade transparency**   MiFID will require that operators of continuous order-matching systems must make aggregated order information available at the five best price levels on the buy and sell side; for quote-driven markets, the best bids and offers of market makers must be made available.
- **Post-trade transparency**   MiFID will require firms to publish the price and volume of all trades, even if executed outside of a regulated market.
- **Best execution**   MiFID will require that firms take all reasonable steps to obtain the best possible result in the execution of an order for a client. The best possible result is not limited to execution price but also includes costs, speed, likelihood of execution, and likelihood of settlement.

(continues)

Continued

- **Systematic internalizer** A systematic internalizer is a firm that executes orders from its clients against its own book or against orders from other clients. MiFID will treat systematic internalizers as mini-exchanges. They will also be subject to pre-trade and post-trade transparency requirements.

12.6 Regulatory and Exchange Reporting

Under the SEC's oversight, self-regulatory organizations (SROs) regulate trading in U.S. equities. The NYSE, the NASD, and regional stock exchanges have set and enforced rules that regulate their members. The cost of market regulation, especially the NASDAQ, has become contentious in recent times. SROs recover market regulation costs from the various market centers that report trades in their listed stocks. These market centers are able to pay these costs from selling real-time trade and quote information in their market to the public.

Increased competition for trading volume has also diminished the effectiveness of market regulation. It is difficult to monitor trading in a stock if the stock trades in multiple markets with different SROs such that each SRO has access to only a part of the audit trail. It is possible for some market centers to dilute their regulatory structure to enhance their competitive advantage. The SEC has been overhauling the current regulatory system.

In November 2006, the NYSE Group Inc and the NASD agreed to form a single regulator for the securities industry. The objective of this accord is to end the rivalry between the NYSE and NASD over how to structure regulatory insight. Bulge-bracket broker-dealers benefit most from the merged entities since they will no longer have to double-report for sometimes overlapping sets of rules. NASD estimated that this could save brokerage firms at least $100 million a year. The venture is expected to begin operating in the second quarter of 2007. The new regulator will oversee securities firms and arbitrate disputes between brokers, clients, and employees. The downside of such a merger is that the competition between arbitration and regulation services will no longer exist. This can potentially hurt institutions and the individual investor. NYSE regulation will retain authority over the more than 2,700 listed companies and over market surveillance at the Big Board and the NYSE Arca electronic options and equity market.

EXAMPLES OF REGULATORY REPORTING

Electronic Blue Sheets Rule

The SEC and SROs use Electronic Blue Sheets to obtain information from broker-dealers to investigate securities law violations such as insider trading or market manipulation. This regulation requires broker-dealers to submit information to regulators upon request regarding customer and firm trading. Electronic blue sheets must be reported within 10 business days of a request regarding data going back up to two prior years. The types of securities that can potentially be requested include stocks and stock options. All exchanges and markets in an equity or option include domestic exchanges, OTC, or international exchanges. Both proprietary trades and customer trades must be reported. The types of transactions include buy, sell, sell short for cash trades, and open, close, long/short positions for options. Cancels must be recorded for both cash trades and options.

Daily Program Trading Report (DPTR)

Members and member firms are required by the NYSE to submit transactions that would qualify as a "program trade." The DPTR must include all program trading data executed both on the NYSE and other markets and regional exchanges. Program trades may be executed during normal market hours or during a special after-hours trading session specifically set aside for the execution of program trades. Member firms are required to submit a report on a daily basis, no later than the close of business on the second business day (T+2). If no program trading occurs on a given trading session, a written report must be submitted to NYSE's market surveillance.

The following key information is required in the DPTR report:

1. Clearing firm #
2. Trade date and time
3. Equity order type and market action
4. Derivative market action
5. Program trade account type
6. Program trade strategy
7. Derivative contract details
8. Multiple record index #
9. NYSE entry method
10. NYSE DOT mnemonic code

SEC 11Ac1-6 Rule

Member firms are required to submit publicly available quarterly reports identifying significant market centers to which nondirected customer orders are routed for execution. The rule also requires brokers to provide details of routing information for customer nondirected orders for the last six months of activity. Member firms are required to make reports publicly available within one month after the end of the quarter. Any national market system security for which there is a transaction report, last sale data, or quotation information is reported. Any listed option contract traded on a national securities exchange for which last sales reports and quotation information must also be reported. The rule requires that the report cover four separate sections for four different types of securities:

1. Equity securities listed on the NYSE
2. Equity securities qualified for inclusion in NASDAQ
3. Equity securities listed on the AMEX or any other national securities exchange
4. Exchange-listed options contracts

Short Interest Rule

Member organizations of the NYSE, AMEX, and NASD must report listed short sale positions held on a monthly basis, with the exception of AMEX, which must report them twice a month. Every member organization must file with the exchange all short positions on a bimonthly basis. The first is due within two business days after the 15th of each month, and the second is due the next business day after the last day of the month. The types of transactions that must be reported include short sells for equities and exchange traded funds. The key items of information required include

1. for NYSE: Bank Identifier, Symbol, Current Short Position;
2. for NASD: Bank Identifier, NASDAQ Security Symbol, Security Name, Current Short Position;
3. for AMEX: Bank Identifier, NASDAQ Security Symbol, Security Name, Current Short Position.

NYSE Rule 123

Members who place exchange orders through a proprietary system are required to report all order and execution details to an exchange-provided database. All details must be time-stamped with the time and date of any reportable event. Order details, modifications, and any cancellations must be preserved for at least three years by an NYSE member. The designated exchange database where orders and executions are submitted is called the Front End System Capture (FESC). The Member Firm Drop Copy (MFDC) is the interface to FESC that transmits order and execution details. Rule 123 reporting is real time and must precede the submission of the actual order.

THE IMPACT OF NMS

Broker-dealers are facing an increase in data acquired from multiple sources, especially from high-speed data services. Regulation NMS allows brokers to compete with exchanges and traditional vendors in selling market data. Brokers who are already increasing their use of data feeds directly from exchanges will now capture the data, aggregate it using their internal systems, and distribute it to their clients. Exchanges will have a greater need to track depth of book and quotes from other ECNs, creating improved data management needs. Regulation NMS will force exchanges to migrate to an all-electronic model and monitor trading activity and execution opportunities at all other competing markets. Most exchanges do not have the capacity to process the volume of quotes that will be needed in a post-regulation NMS world.

12.7 Example of an Exchange Data Processing System

The designated NYSE database to which order and execution data is submitted is called the Front End System Capture (FESC). The Member Firm Drop Copy (MFDC) is the interface to FESC that transmits order and execution details. The Member Firm Drop Copy is the interface application where reports are submitted to FESC.

The following different types of events require drop copies sent to FESC:

1. Orders before they get accepted by the trader/clerk on the floor
2. Orders after they get accepted on the floor
3. Rejects
4. Cancels
5. Corrections
6. All floor executions not forwarded to DOT, BBSS, and CAP-DI from the floor
7. Execution corrections
8. Execution busts (a canceled trade due to an error on the exchange side)

MFDC has been implemented to support member firms' compliance with the modifications made to NYSE Rule 123. The MDFC application receives drop copy messages (in electronic form) from member firms for processing and forwarding to the FESC database. The NYSE CAP network is an "extranet" infrastructure that serves as a common point of access between the NYSE production networks and the networks of member firms. MFDC application is responsible for the receipt and storage of all information sent by the member firms as they comply with Rule 123. Drop copies are transmitted via the NYSE Common Access Point (CAP) network and then processed by MFDC. The FESC service processes, inserts, and updates the MFDC database in accordance with Rule 123. The FESC database forms the repository of the drop copy data that NYSE market surveillance monitors to verify member firm compliance. Drop copies are copies of orders, reports, and modifications thereof, transmitted to the FESC system via the proprietary OMSs of the member firms. All member firm orders and order modifications sent to the floor via their proprietary OMS are required to be captured in the FESC database. Regardless of the firm's origination point for the copies of the orders and reports, delivery of the drop copy shall be via NYSE CAP network to the MDFC application interface of the FESC.

The exchanges will need to convert all their systems to an electronic format in order to improve their routing facilities. This is due in large part to their need to track the activity at all of the other exchanges and route away to firms that have better prices. Member firms will need to change the way they handle increased data volumes to satisfy regulatory requirements and also must be able to execute potentially profitable trading opportunities. Speed is more critical than ever as markets accentuate the growing volume of data. The sharply growing volume of market data will continue to increase as a result of regulation NMS; trading institutions that have an infrastructure capable of storing all of the necessary data and analyzing it in real time can be most assured of meeting their best execution goals. Network capacity will continue to grow in expectation of an increase in market data. The largest broker-dealers will be required to store and analyze a significant increase in market data facilitated by substantial changes to their technology infrastructures.[4]

12.8 Conclusion

The implementation of Regulation NMS will modernize and strengthen the National Market System (NMS). Reg NMS is focused on the following areas of market structure and regulation: the "Order Protection or New

---

[4] Robert Iati, *Reg NMS: Driving the Urgency for Data Storage*, TABB Group Report, November 2005: 3–4, http://www.tabbgroup.com/our_reports.php?tabbaction=4&reportId=122.

Trade-Through Rule," the "Access Rule," the "Sub-Penny Rule," and the "Market Data Rules." The impact on the sell side for the Order Protection Rule is the need for brokers to update their order management systems to route orders to multiple marketplaces and to execute them against liquidity at several price points. This rule can potentially eliminate the role of the NYSE floor brokers who are given large institutional orders in reserve; under the new rule, hidden reserves or better-priced orders will now be exposed. This rule will provide more liquidity as the buy side will display its limit orders. The Access Rule will have limited impact on sell-side firms given that most broker-dealers already have private linkages. Traditional buy-side firms are oblivious to access fees given that they pay brokerage firms to absorb all underlying costs. The Sub-Penny Rule has little impact on the sell side. Traditional buy-side firms will likely favor the proposal because hedge funds will no longer be allowed to quote in sub-pennies used to jump ahead of their limit orders. The Market Data Rules will provide relief for the sell side from having the burden of displaying quotes from all market centers trading a particular security. Brokers will benefit from more efficient use of systems and more easily extract necessary data. The buy side will be able to pay for only the data they use.

Chapter 13

Build vs. Buy

13.1 Introduction

Broker dealers and exchanges have been under intense pressure to stream-line entire trading processes to reduce transaction costs and improve quality of execution while limiting risk. Throughout the 1990s, the financial community assumed that the only effective way to trade electronically with clients is by building a proprietary trading platform. This assumption gave control for the owner in terms of dealing logic, instrument specification, customization, and enhancements. It was critical for large broker-dealers to differentiate themselves from their competition and outsourcing was clearly not appropriate. Outsourced vendors lacked the personal relationships and organizational context to support complex business strategies.[1] As a result, brokers spent millions on trading systems only to find them over budget, with deliverables that do not meet deadlines, and also outdated by the time they are deployed. Brokers also neglected to factor total cost of ownership from ongoing enhancements, development, and supporting additional assets or instruments. Trading firms and other automated trading operations today are always on the lookout for newer, faster technology; the adoption of new technology is rarely a simple, efficient process. The real cost is connecting to all the applications and the rest of the technology infrastructure. Costs such as licensing fees are usually only a small consideration of the overall cost of

---

[1] Sarah Keys, "Online Trading Platforms: To Build or to Buy?" *Commodities Now*, September 2002: 1–3.

vendor-provided technology. Several issues had to be addressed in deciding whether or not to build or buy a trading platform. The history of automated trading can be clearly traced in the trading process progressing to what it is today (see Exhibit 13.1):

- **High touch trading:** Prices are quoted over the phone.
- **Indicative prices:** Prices are published but require manual confirmation.
- **Screen-based-trading:** Prices can be executed on a screen.
- **Automated trading:** Prices can be published and executed by a computer.

Automated trading originated with vendors providing execution data on the exchange floors and other trading venues. Originally, vendors were simply data providers, but under competitive pressure, they were allowed to publish tradable prices on vendor quotation screens, and finally were enabled to engage in electronic automated trading. In the past couple of years, vendors such as Reuters, EBS, and Bloomberg have been trading across all the underlying instruments, which include equities, foreign exchange, and fixed-income instruments.

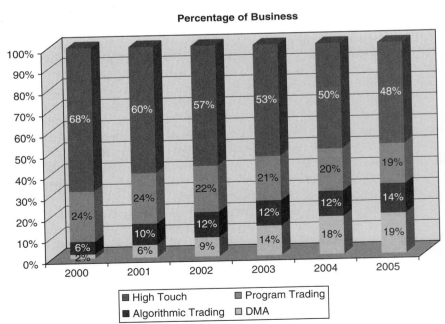

Exhibit 13.1   *Source:* Broker-dealers, Aite Group estimates.

In order to integrate pre-trade through post-trade analytics, brokers have not only been adopting vendor relationships but are buying up these ECN aggregators all together. Prime examples of this phenomenon are Goldman Sachs acquiring Speer Leads & Kellogg (SLK), a specialist, which owns the ECN aggregator REDIPlus, and Citigroup acquiring Lava Trading, the largest of the institutionally favored aggregators. Other transactions include the March 2004 acquisition of Direct Access Financial Corporation by Banc of America Securities and the March 2004 purchase of Sonic Financial Technologies by the Bank of New York Securities.[2] ECN aggregators allow traders to achieve execution efficiency through

- quickly assessing the market for an equity using a single aggregated screen on a desktop;
- shifting more of their order flow to automated trading, allowing them to concentrate on value-added trades such as less liquid small-cap stocks or private placements;
- connecting to all liquidity sources;
- easily integrating program trading tools;
- easily integrating with algorithmic and analytic tools.[3]

In September 2005, Investment Technology Group (ITG), a leading provider of technology-based equity trading services and transaction research, acquired the Plexus Group, Inc., a Los Angeles–based firm dedicated to enhancing investment performance. The Plexus Group was previously a subsidiary of JP Morgan Chase Bank. "This acquisition expands the breadth of ITG's analytical products and increases the range of our client base. ITG is dedicated to helping customers better navigate an increasingly complex marketplace. The combination of Plexus Group's consultative approach to transaction cost analysis with ITG's reputation for superior technology, customer service, and support will allow ITG to provide a comprehensive transaction cost analysis solution to a wider marketplace," stated Ray Killian, ITG's Chairman, President, and Chief Executive Officer.

13.2 Vendor as a Service Provider

The securities industry has been dictated by consolidation. This has been driven by the recent recession after the Internet bust; regulation such as decimalization, which has undermined the traditional spread-based business

---

[2] Lori Master, White Paper: "ECN Aggregators—Increasing Transparency and Liquidity in Equity Markets," *Random Walk Computing*, Fall 2004: 6–8.
[3] Ibid.: 12.

model; and new trading venues. Downsized development teams are asked to rebuild applications and infrastructure on tight schedules. According to Larry Tabb, CEO of the TABB Group, "Economics are pushing banks away from proprietary development, to using more vendor-based products and finally consolidating their vendor relationships around unique and strategic vendors." The proliferation of the FIX protocol has made it possible for independent software vendors to provide destination-neutral systems for electronic trading. The pressure of increased competition and consolidation has resulted in internal IT departments that cannot keep up to date with meeting the needs of an increasingly demanding market within budget. The advantages of buying or outsourcing from neutral software developers include the following:

- A quicker time-to-market.
- A desire to focus resources on core competencies.
- Ease of integration with third-party technology.
- Cost savings in maintenance (companies often underestimate how much time can be spent maintaining internally developed solutions; as employees who created the applications leave, maintenance becomes more difficult).
- High reliability through battle-tested, proven performance with robust APIs for seamless integration. (An application programming interface [API] is the interface that a computer system, library, or application provides in order to allow requests for services to be made of it by other computer programs and/or to allow data to be exchanged between them.)
- Ability to draw on a broad range of expertise from proven developers.[4]

A vendor option for the buy side is to utilize a broker-provided algorithm. A broker-provided system requires minimum technological infrastructure on the client side to access execution models. It can provide a wider range of advanced algorithms, which rely on research, infrastructure, and maintenance costs. This includes compiled historical data, computer hardware, and network infrastructure to deal with a considerable amount of real-time market data. The risk of utilizing a broker algorithm is higher risk of information leakage, and for brokers to use the client's historical trade data to predict future trade events used for their own purposes. Brokers also charge higher commission rates and utilize fewer algorithmic parameters to end users.[5]

---

[4] Sarah Keys, "Online Trading Platforms: To Build or to Buy?" *Commodities Now*, September 2002: 1–3.
[5] Allen Zaydin, "Build or Buy?" in *Algorithmic Trading: A Buy-Side Handbook*, 29–31 (London: The Trade Ltd., 2005).

The evolution of trading technology has allowed the buy side to take increasing control of their trading environment with tools such as ECNs, direct market access (DMA) systems, crossing networks, and algorithmic trading. The proliferation of the Financial Information Exchange (FIX), the industry protocol adopted by the buy side and sell side to communicate orders electronically, has enhanced productivity for the buy side through interfacing with multiple dealers and finding alternative sources for liquidity. Order Management Systems (OMSs) are the central part for integrating front, middle, and back offices where the buy-side trader collects orders from portfolio managers, aggregates them into blocks, and performs allocations. It is unclear how OMSs will handle more complex algorithms, particularly as algorithms move beyond equities where OMSs will then need to support cross-asset-class algorithmic trades. The use of OMSs has led to major improvements in trade execution efficiencies, but OMS providers have mainly offered algorithmic trading support primarily through integration with a broker's remote algorithms or third-party platforms. OMS vendors currently control the desktops of buy-side trading desks. Broker-dealers see ECN aggregators and OMSs as a crucial part of extending relationships with the buy side. The buy side typically wants neutrality and is willing to develop their own proprietary OMS for their desktops. In order for this to be achieved, the buy side typically needs to come up with a source independent of their brokers. There is a constant struggle for brokers trying to maintain soft dollar contracts with the buy side providing research in return for execution business. The buy-side trader on the contrary is trying to demonstrate the best execution methodologies. In order for the buy side to attain broker neutrality, their OMS needs to come from a source that is independent of their brokers. An in-house OMS can potentially provide neutrality as well as integrating with other analytic programs developed in-house. In the late 90s Macgregor became the first OMS to offer their own proprietary order-routing network, called MFN. Denise Valentine, an analyst at Celent Communication, comments: "MFN is the oldest OMS, other competitors are launching similar financial networks. Charles River is launching one, FMC has FMCNet in Canada which is coming to the U.S., and SunGard has the SunGard Transaction Network (STN)." In July 2005, ITG officially announced a definitive agreement to acquire privately held Macgregor, a leading provider of trade order management technology for the global financial community. The combined entities will provide clients with a best-execution order management system that will closely integrate real-time data, analytics, order management, and execution tools into a complete solution for institutional trading desks. The transaction ended months of speculation surrounding a possible sale of the Boston-based OMS provider. Macgregor's software is a central hub for trading used by 100 blue-chip institutional clients including Babson Capital, Delaware Investments, and T. Rowe Price with about $5.5 trillion in assets. Rumors circulated that Reuters, SunGard, and Thomson Financial were among the bidders for Macgregor, according to industry sources.[6] Broker neutrality will remain an important element in acquiring other order management systems. Steven Levy, president and CEO of Macgregor, says, "It is important to note that your broker neutrality and anonymity requirements will continue to be held paramount. You will continue to be able to trade with any broker and liquidity venue you chose." This may possibly be the beginning trend of broker-dealers acquiring order management systems.

The purchase of an order management system involves several departments. These include IT, trading, portfolio management, compliance, and operations. Important considerations should be made. The following basic outline illustrates a checklist to consider in purchasing a vendor OMS.

- **Product price**   Order management systems are bought or leased. Some vendors offer both options. If the system is purchased, expect a higher initial outlay, with monthly maintenance fees often as high as 20–25% of the initial cost. Leased systems incur higher monthly premiums, but come with lower initial cost. Hidden charges may appear, such as substantial installation and integration costs.
- **Implementation process**   Implementation of an order management system often takes 3 to 6 months. The complexity of the installation and the vendor's number of current or pending implementations often dictate implementation time. The best benchmark with the installation process is contacting other clients about their installation experience.
- **Support**   Some order management systems are complex and require the investment manager to have a sophisticated IT department, while others are easier to install and maintain. Be sure to balance the sophistication of your IT staff with the technical expertise required by the OMS. Some OMS vendors are willing to take on these IT requirements. Many OMS firms are small and may not have the resources for an effective support staff. Again, the best benchmark is to check with other clients about their support experience.
- **Third-party interfaces and data sharing**   Firms need to think about how they will interact with the markets. Will they use crossing networks, algorithms, ECNs, DMAs, or FIX to connect to brokers? The OMS must be integrated with a portfolio management system, execution venues, accounting system, risk management, and other systems

---

6 Ivy Schmerken, "ITG to Acquire Macgregor OMS Business and Financial Network," *Finance Tech*, July 14, 2005.

that require trade data. If an OMS does not have an interface, the vendor will offer to build one for a fee. Be aware that beta users for a custom interface often involve a lot of time on the investment manager's part.

- **Transaction cost analysis integration**   Transaction cost analysis (TCA) tools analyze a firm's executions by comparing them to specific benchmarks. These analytics try to analyze market impact, compare the trade execution to the portfolio manager's instructions, and examine the executions in conjunction with various portfolio or firm benchmarks.[7]

13.3 Striving to Stand Out

Algorithmic trading consists of a system that collects market data and analyzes this information, executing trades established by a set of strategies. The introduction of ECNs along with the buy side's demand for better execution has prompted broker-dealers to enhance their electronic trading capabilities in order to remain competitive for buy-side business and soft dollar expenditure. In an attempt to retain market share, broker-dealers began offering clients direct market access and algorithmic technology. The sell side inadvertently shot themselves in the foot as once-proprietary order-routing technology became more and more accessible to the buy side. Broker-dealers in return have been acquiring ECN aggregators in order to retain market share.

A successful algorithmic trade results in massive quantities of real-time market data properly streamlined through systems. The primary concern is the speed of this data. A millisecond (1/1,000 of a second) can differentiate between a successful trade and an unsuccessful trade. Slow market data (difference of a few hundred milliseconds) can mean successfully executing via one system while losing opportunity to profit via another. One way of differentiating from one system is through reducing the delay in the transmission of information. One way of accomplishing this is the elimination of the middleman. The best way of aggregating data and providing it to customers for an algorithmic platform provider is getting market data feeds directly from the source. This model will potentially be faster since data is making one less stop on its journey. Electronic trading groups and proprietary traders increasingly need direct exchange feeds instead of consolidated market data feeds provided by data vendors such as Reuters or Bloomberg. According to Vijay Kedia, president of Flextrade: "Latency is

---

[7] Wendy Dailey, *Order Management Systems*, Capital Institutional Services, Inc., Fourth Quarter 2005, http://www.capis.com/CAPIS%20OMS%202005.pdf.

an important issue as the data itself. Anyone who gets data straight from the source finds an immediate shortcut." Flextrade now gets all of its feeds straight from the source, such as the NYSE, NASDAQ, and ECNs.[8]

Brokerage firms are struggling to differentiate themselves as electronic trading becomes more commonplace. According to the Aite Group, approximately 28% of total equities trading volume were executed algorithmically in 2005, versus 25% in 2004. Sell-side desks are shrinking and being held responsible for cutting costs while retaining business as more ECN aggregators appear on institutional buy-side desks. We are seeing a great number of acquisitions of direct-access firms by broker-dealers. This is the result of buy-side traders integrating more black box technology, and the utilization of a direct market access platform such as an ECN aggregator. The proliferation of the FIX protocol has allowed the buy side to use an ECN aggregator and algorithmic trading programs without establishing a relationship with the sell side via a phone order. The buy side has become increasingly shrewder about accessing markets directly without the help of brokerage firms. Large brokerage firms in return are spending millions each year to better their algorithmic trading offerings and relevant technology. Broker-dealers are also developing algorithms that not only appeal to U.S. domestic equities markets, but for other asset classes as well. Clients will look for trading solutions that address issues such as accessing global markets as well as multiple asset classes.

BROKER-PROVIDED ALGORITHMS VS. VENDOR-PROVIDED BROKER-NEUTRAL ALGORITHMS

Typically a broker-provided algorithm will charge $0.0075 per share as a common rate. A firm trading one million shares per month will pay approximately $7,500 per month in commission fees. At the same time a firm must also pay to have DMA connect to a broker-neutral algorithm, which can charge around $0.0015 per share. If a typical broker-neutral algorithmic provider charges $10,000 per month fixed cost for unlimited trades, then paying $7,500 for a broker-provided algorithm from a sell-side firm is clearly cheaper and advantageous if a client does not care about information leakage as opposed to paying $11,500 for a broker-neutral system. The break-even point between spending the same amount for a broker-provided algorithm as opposed to utilizing a broker-neutral system is approximately 1.5 million shares per month. The larger the average number of shares a firm

---

[8] Patrick Burke, April 2006, "Miles from the Curb, IT Recruiting on Wall Street: Algorithmic Trading," http://patrickburke1980.typepad.com/main/2006/04/algo_trading.html (last accessed February 6, 2007).

trades, the more advantageous a broker-neutral algorithm becomes. This theory will only hold true, however, if both broker-provider and broker-neutral provider deliver the same performance.[9]

13.4 The Surge of Electronic Trading Through Regulatory Changes

The introduction of Regulation NMS will require markets to become quicker and will allow traders to enhance speed of execution for the best price. The regulatory changes will require better electronic linkages between all markets, entitling investors with the best prices as long as orders could be filed automatically. Acquisitions and mergers between exchanges and ECNs have been occurring in anticipation of the regulatory changes. The speed of message traffic as a result of Reg NMS is expected to increase 50–300% in the upcoming years. Firms are expected to significantly increase spending to process additional data. Additional information will be needed to execute orders in subseconds, promoting more electronic trading. In order to get the data, the sell side will contract vendors, buy quote feeds directly from exchanges, or use their own technology. The broker-dealers will need the data to prove that they offer the best execution on orders. The research firm TowerGroup projects that market data spending will increase by 7% each year eventually reaching $4.3 billion in 2008. Total IT spending will increase by about 3% each year in comparison (see Exhibit 13.2).[10]

13.5 Hedge Fund Systems—Outsource or In-House?

The advantages for a hedge fund in using an algorithm for trade execution are clear. Managers can potentially have the ability to place large orders anonymously without tipping off the market. There is no doubt that algorithms and direct market access present a significant advantage over personalized phone trades, offering lower cost of execution, forcing broker-dealers to adapt offering better execution venues. The danger however, is not the cost of the execution itself, but how the execution is handled. A poorly handled algorithm can allow an outsider to peek in at a proprietary strategy. Hedge funds are also leery of their brokers. The sell-side broker can

[9] Allen Zaydin, "Build or Buy?" in *Algorithmic Trading: A Buy-Side Handbook*, 29–31 (London: The Trade Ltd., 2005).
[10] Veronica Belitski, "Brokerages Strive to Stand Out Amid Algo Glut," *Electronic Trading Outlook, Wall Street Letter*, June 2006, http://www.rblt.com/documents/hybridsupplement.pdf.

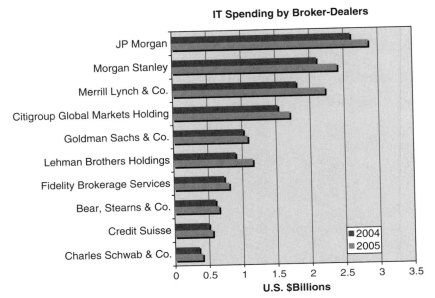

IT Spending by Broker-Dealers

Exhibit 13.2   *Source:* Company filings, interviews, Aite Group.

potentially use algorithmic orders for their own purposes, going against the buy-side execution (see Exhibit 13.3). Agency-only brokers may pose less of a risk than large broker-dealers, given that many do not have proprietary trading desks trading firm capital on behalf of the bank. In the end, the buy-side trader needs to trust the avenue in which he/she chooses to execute an order. In response to this, brokerage firms are increasingly displaying their algorithms on multiple broker-neutral execution management systems. This allows the buy-side trader to access multiple liquidity pools as well as leverage a wide variety of algorithms. The way to minimize risk is by using Volume-Weighted Average Price (VWAP) or Time-Weighted Average Price (TWAP) techniques. A VWAP or TWAP approach can allow for a random price that does not affect the market. Poor algorithms can also feed bad data into the system where orders get misfired, causing portfolio managers to be long when they should be short. One of the biggest factors for the growth of algorithmic trading has been increased awareness of execution costs, the growth of hedge funds, and advancements of automation.

Hedge funds have many outsourcing options. They can develop their own algorithm, customize an existing one provided by a vendor, and also out-source their operations department. There is a large and increasing array of execution tools offered by software vendors and brokers. There are some managers who even outsource their entire front-office execution function to

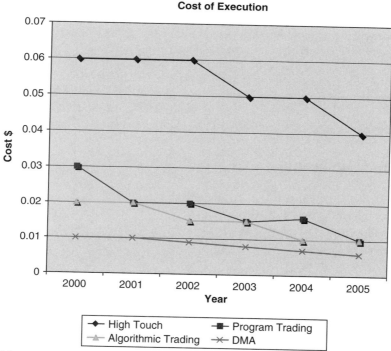

Cost of Execution

Legend:
- High Touch
- Program Trading
- Algorithmic Trading
- DMA

Exhibit 13.3   *Source:* Broker-dealers, Aite Group estimates.

specialists. Middle- and back-office outsourcing has also grown tremendously. This typically includes the handling of trade confirmations, corporate actions, pricing, general ledger, and investor services. Broker-dealers provide lucrative services such as prime brokerage, which allows hedge funds to take leverage on their positions providing equity. Hedge funds also outsource their back-office functions to satisfy more stringent regulations assessing their compliance capabilities so they can better manage their internal processes. Fierce competition among brokers and software providers is presenting more outsourcing opportunities.

The business complexity of a hedge fund can play a crucial role in deciding whether or not to outsource. For example, a long/short equity portfolio is relatively simple to support from both a software and operational perspective. The converse is true for hedge funds that invest significantly in debt portfolios, and fixed-income strategies. These markets are more illiquid, and outsourced staff may not have the aptitude or have the organizational context to handle such orders efficiently.

The decision to outsource for a hedge fund depends on how it can be utilized to one's competitive advantage. Some managers who focus their investment strategy in derivatives or multicurrency assets will want to utilize a proprietary model. Outsourcing is clearly not appropriate in this instance where judgment needs to be made. Most fund managers are interested in growth. This has significant implications in deciding whether or not to outsource, and if so, which software to deploy. If the intention is to increase staff and trading volume, as well as venture into different asset classes, a scalable in-house software solution may be the answer.

13.6 Conclusion

The sell side will continue to undertake the difficult task of maintaining strong relationships with the buy side, which will allow them to grasp a foothold on market share. Major broker-dealers will enhance their market data infrastructure in order to translate large quantities of real-time data demanded by algorithmic and other automated trading systems for best execution. This will eliminate as much latency as possible. Direct market access companies, OMSs, and ECN aggregators will continue to be acquired by broker-dealers. Individual investors will put further pressure on their brokers and mutual fund managers for more transparency and to better understand management and operation fees. ECN aggregation is a natural progression and will continue to pressure the competition for desk space for the buy-side trader. The sell side may soon come to the conclusion that selling trading technology solutions may generate income streams that are parallel with traditional trading commissions. This will further motivate broker-dealers to acquire direct market access firms and OMS capabilities. The equity side has evolved considerably with algorithmic trading. It may not be long before the fixed-income side catches up. For the buy side, algorithms are a high fixed-cost, low-variable cost method of trading. The high cost of development and testing of algorithmic strategies will keep most buy-side development of algorithmic trading strategies to a minimum. In addition to development, participating in an arms race to enhance and upgrade the algorithms would be a significant resources drain on buy-side firms in a market where, due to the low-variable cost, brokers offer the service at less than premium commission rates. Implementation of an algorithm into a high throughput, fast trading infrastructure is as important as the algorithm itself.[11]

---

[11] Ary Khatchikian et al., "Algorithmic Trading: The State of Algo Trading," *Waters*, Special Reports March 2006, http://www.watersonline.com/public/showPage.html?page=318491.

Chapter 14

Trading Technology and Prime Brokerage

14.1 Introduction

Trading and technology have led to several new developments. Electronic trading has reduced the amount of human interaction, and radically changed the nature of the roles that the buy side and sell side play in the workflow. Firms are increasingly using "black box" trading in the investment decision process. According to the TABB Group, black box refers to computer programs that focus on a combination of real-time market data and fundamentals to derive buy and sell signals. Mathematicians or "quants" have programs capable of analyzing large amounts of financial data, which allow them to profit from small gains made off brief imbalances in the market. The rise of black box trading has significantly increased the number of trades. Trade technology has led to several developments such as direct market access (DMA) and algorithmic trading, enabling investment professionals to expedite the trade process.[1]

Prime brokers provide technological support, ensure access to markets, develop synthetic products, and provide operational functions for settlements, custody, and reporting for buy-side trades. The main reason why prime brokers carry out custody activity is to facilitate margin-lending

---

[1] Adam Sussman, *Managing Risk in Real-Time Markets*, Tabb Group Report, February 2005, http://www.tabbgroup.com/our_reports.php?tabbaction=4&reportId=87.

activities and the associated movement of collateral. Prime brokers earn their revenue through cash lending to support leverage and stock lending to facilitate short selling. It is increasingly common for prime broker clients to structure trades, utilizing synthetic products and other different asset classes. In the stock-lending business, prime brokers act as an intermediary between institutional lenders and other hedge fund borrowers. In financing equity role, prime brokers act in the role of an intermediary.

14.2 Prime Broker Services

The services that a prime broker provides include the following (see Exhibit 14.1):

1. **Margin management**   To calculate margin requirements by clients across positions. New stand-alone systems can track margin requirements in real time and aggregate them across instruments and markets.
2. **Securities lending**   To monitor the availability of borrowing rates for lending securities as well as to handle the process of new transactions, rollovers, and redemptions.
3. **Clearance and settlements**   To support reconciliation of trades along with clearance and settlement through industry utilities.
4. **Execution access**   The need for real-time electronic access to brokers and ECNs so that trades can be captured efficiently.
5. **Automated confirmation and reconciliation**   Middle offices of hedge funds need real-time electronic confirmations of executed trades and reconciliation of settlement instructions across all transactions. The principal focus is on efficiency and elimination of errors and costs associated with manual reconciliations.
6. **Integrated daily position reporting**   Hedge funds need a recap of all trades executed in a fund during a given day, resulting in end-of-day position, in order to facilitate reconciliation of a net position and track gross performance.

When a hedge fund enters into a prime brokerage relationship, it is given access to a reserve of securities that the prime broker has in custody at any given time. The reserve or "box" may be from the brokerage's customer accounts, or it may be borrowed from a custodian such as State Street. Hedge funds are given a credit rating, then a margin account, that allows them to borrow cash up to a certain amount to make a trade. The application that manages credit limits, also called the "margin engine," exists downstream in the chain of processing events. The margin engine usually requests information from another application or database for the inputs to its calculation. This calculation will become increasingly inaccurate as more

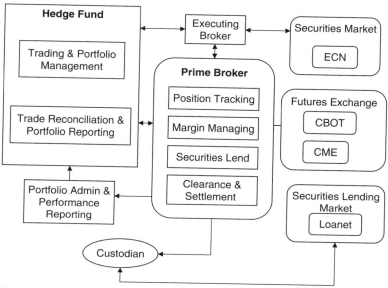

Exhibit 14.1   Hedge Fund Execution Flow.

transactions occur. The bottleneck that prevents firms from implementing the ideal margin calculation is the limitations in retrieving information required to perform the calculations, according to the TABB Group. Open orders are usually stored in one database and the current trade positions are stored in another. The margin engine must perform two separate queries to perform the calculation.

Securities lending is the process of one firm owning an asset and agreeing to lend it to another firm at a fixed or variable interest rate. Assets are usually held with a custodian. Custodians will lend assets to the prime broker on demand, conditional upon the prime broker's guarantee that the security will not be lost or hurt. Prime brokers typically lend this security to the open market. Typically, the securities lending desk at a broker-dealer is responsible for setting the rebate rate, which is the interest rate that a bank will pay a hedge fund for leaving cash on collateral to borrow the stock. This rebate rate can vary significantly. Easy-to-borrow stocks have positive rebate rates, which means a bank will pay a hedge fund for their cash, while hard-to-borrow stocks may have negative interest rates, which means the hedge fund must pay the broker interest in order to borrow the stock. According to the Aite Group, the economics of securities lending and margin accounts are based on capturing the spread. When a broker or bank lends money so hedge funds can trade on margin, they are paid an interest rate that is typically the federal funds rate plus 40 basis points.[2] In September 2005, the fed funds rate was 3.75% per year; today's margin rates are 4.15%.

Commercial banks in the past were usually unwilling to take credit exposure directly to all but the largest hedge funds, but this is beginning to change. Prime brokers' margining practices vary, but essentially, they aim to ensure that in the event that a hedge fund client defaults on a loan, they are able to cover the full amount through the sale of the collateral assets. As the number of trades increase, it becomes harder for prime brokers to manage credit limits and calculate market risk. In December 2004, 50% of hedge funds used low leverage, 20% did not use leverage at all, while 30% used high leverage (see Exhibit 14.2). On average, hedge funds have borrowed eighty cents on the dollar in assets. Prime brokerage has traditionally been dominated by niche players in the past, but larger banks are increasingly getting

Strategy	Do Not Use	Low (<2.0:1)	High (=>2.0:1)
Aggressive Growth	20%	60%	20%
Emerging Markets	20	50%	30%
Equity Market Neutral	15%	50%	35%
Event Driven	15%	60%	25%
Income	35%	30%	35%
Macro	10%	30%	60%
Market Neutral Arbitrage	10%	25%	65%
Market Timing	55%	35%	10%
Multi-Strategy	10%	50%	40%
Opportunistic	10%	60%	30%
Short Selling	30%	40%	30%
Value	20%	60%	20%

Exhibit 14.2 Global hedge funds' use of leverage. *Source:* Van Hedge Fund Advisors, Aite Group.

---

[2] Sang Lee, "Shaking Up Prime Brokerage: Unbundling Securities Lending, Financing, and Derivatives Transactions," Aite Group Report 200510171 (October 2005): 9–10.

into fund servicing. Large banks figure this is an easy way to gain a foothold in global reach, technology, and personnel capabilities that smaller players cannot.

14.3 The Structure of Hedge Funds

Hedge funds today have grown to more than $1.225 trillion in assets under management by the end of the second quarter of 2006 according to the recently released data by Chicago-based Hedge Fund Research Inc. (HFR). They are increasingly becoming mainstream. Higher returns are clearly attracting assets, investor interest, and professional talent. The investment objective for buy-side firms such as hedge funds is to provide investors with superior long-term capital appreciation through buying undervalued instruments and simultaneously selling overvalued ones. Hedge funds typically do not follow any established approach. They usually focus their expertise on identifying arbitrage opportunities. The term "hedge fund" applies to a broader range of strategies than pure arbitrage. Some hedge funds focus on purely directional bets through high-quality trade information monitoring changes in investor sentiment. The advent of hedge funds saw fundamental changes in the structure of financial markets. First, the markets became more transparent as advances in information technology allowed exchanges and Electronic Communication Networks (ECNs) to provide vastly more detailed market information at low cost. Second, specialized providers such as prime brokerage began offering efficient access to markets with low-cost clearing and settlement. For example, execution costs for equity trades have dropped over 75% over the last five years.

Hedge funds tend to outsource everything except portfolio construction and trading. Typically investors will provide capital to the hedge fund. Hedge funds will invest through two kinds of brokers: "prime brokers" and "executing brokers." The executing broker provides access to the markets. The prime broker keeps track of all transactions and provides financing for leverage positions. The "fund administrator," typically a custodian or specialized third party, will manage the fund's books of records and produce monthly portfolio and performance reports for the fund itself and for each investor (see Exhibit 14.3).

Typically, hedge funds start out with system requirements, which include the following functions:

- Administrative and legal support to handle contracts with investors and manage the funding process
- Market data and analytics to identify arbitrage opportunities and for portfolio tracking and risk management
- Trade reconciliation through a prime broker to track clearance and settlement

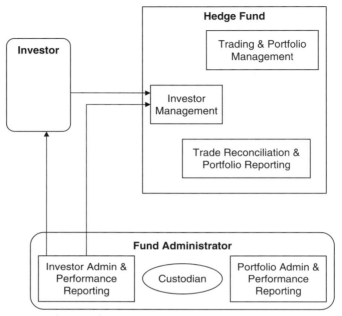

Exhibit 14.3   Hedge Fund Reporting.

- Financing of inventory, securities borrowing and margin management through the prime broker
- Trade and portfolio analytics to model price and evaluate transactions and strategies
- Access to securities lending markets to provide direct connectivity to lenders through securities lending networks
- Risk management to run and monitor portfolio and aggregate risks
- Performance reporting and risk attribution to compute performance records of each strategy, fund, and fund family and provide risk-adjusted return reports to investors independently from the fund administrator.[3]

14.4 The Impact of Increased Trading Automation

Automation has led to an increase in both trades and market data, challenging the infrastructure at hedge funds and prime brokers. The TABB Group estimates that during peak cycles, top-tier prime brokers could be hit with close to 150 trades per second and more than 10 times as

---

[3] Sungard, "The Emergence of Hedge Funds," *SungardWorld* 3 no. 1, http://www.sungard.com/company_info/v311623.pdf.

many orders per second, imposing a tremendous expense on the applications that must update and disseminate this data. Hedge funds, which typically execute orders at a rapid pace, draw their credit relationships with prime brokers. Hedge funds borrow money from prime brokers under margining agreements, which require the hedge funds to deposit cash and securities as collateral for trades. However, many prime brokers trade on different electronic platforms, choosing multiple execution brokers for lower commissions, expertise, or more effective algorithms. Prime brokers have the challenge of effectively picking up all these trades in the back office. Each time a trade occurs, the prime broker's system must immediately update the accounts' positions stored in their databases. Prime brokers can be incurring more risks because they are not calculating margin deposits in real time. When a broker cannot calculate trading limits as fast as its clients are placing orders, one of two undesirable scenarios can occur: Either the prime broker imposes conservative margin requirements, which limit trading, or the firm allows the trading to occur but takes on additional counterparty risk. When prime brokers impose conservative margin requirements (which occurs when a firm implements highly conservative credit or margin calculations to protect against active accounts), the margin is constrained by the cash in the account. This prevents the firm from taking on counterparty risk at the expense of the client's ability to trade. Usually hedge funds that use DMA, black box models, or algorithms trade high volume, which generates more commissions, so few prime brokers are willing to impose conservative margin requirements for these clients.

14.5 Different Markets and Asset Classes

Hedge funds are continuing to apply more proactive strategies across different markets and products. Hedge fund managers and other alternative investment professionals fear that investors will put more money in traditional products such as mutual funds if the fund's return on investment is not above its standard benchmark. As funds begin to apply strategies across different markets, the prime broker's responsibility in managing credit limits, and monitoring risk becomes harder.

The second most important source of income for prime brokers according to the Aite Group is derivative transactions. These include swaps and other custom transactions that allow a hedge fund to gain exposure to a particular sector or geography without the cost and expense of buying securities in the open market. Aite Group research suggests that on average, a prime broker or bank earns between 0.5% in revenues on a hedge fund's assets under management. The global notional value of open over-the-counter derivatives transactions (including banks, brokers industry, and hedge funds) is U.S. $248 trillion (see Exhibit 14.4) according to the Bank for International Settlements (BIS).

As hedge funds gather more assets, they push toward investments that are less liquid called "side pockets." These tend to be investments that are hard to value. Many funds have approximately 5% of their total portfolio in side pockets with some funds increasing that figure to 10–15%. As funds begin to push more side pockets, they begin to operate as a private equity fund. Side pockets raise the question regarding how the fund values its NAV. Typically, the value is left at cost until their estimated fair market values change significantly. Fund managers usually receive allocation and performance fees when those assets are eventually sold, which can create a conflict of interest among investors. A poorly performing side pocket may drive down the fund's NAV, but the fund's partners will receive a performance based-fee based on positive returns for larger liquid portions within the portfolio.

As computing power becomes cheaper, with greater transparency across different asset classes, investment products such as fixed-income instruments and foreign exchange will progress toward bigger pools of electronic liquidity. As this occurs, the TABB Group expects more hedge funds and alternative investment vehicles to trade these asset classes.

14.6 The Prime Brokerage Market

From the broker perspective, revenues are estimated to be $17.2 billion USD ($12.2 billion USD for securities lending and $5 billion USD for

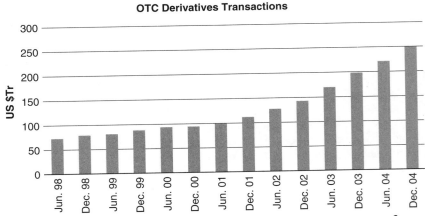

OTC Derivatives Transactions

Exhibit 14.4 Notional value of outstanding OTC derivative transactions. *Source:* Bank for International Settlements, Aite Group.

derivatives). This estimate seems optimistic, with the Aite Group estimating that figure to be closer to $10 billion USD for securities lending and about $5 billion USD for derivative transactions.[4] In 2004, Goldman Sachs earned $1.3 billion USD in securities service; for 2005, this estimate increases to $1.7 billion USD or about 10% of all global hedge fund prime brokerage service (see Exhibit 14.5). In comparison, Bear Stearns' 2004 revenues for Global Clearing Services were $921 million USD (see Exhibit 14.6). Bear Stearns' revenue for 2005 is estimated to be over $1 billion USD or 7% of the industry.

IT spending within fund administrators and prime brokerage is currently around $140 million and estimated to increase to $250 million by 2008, according to the TowerGroup. Fidelity Investments routinely spends more than $2 billion annually for fund administrators, so IT spending seems very moderate.

14.7 Conclusion

The core business of prime brokerage is simple in concept. A prime broker clears and settles trades, keeps custody, and lends capital against assets, providing leverage. They also maintain books and records. A distinct

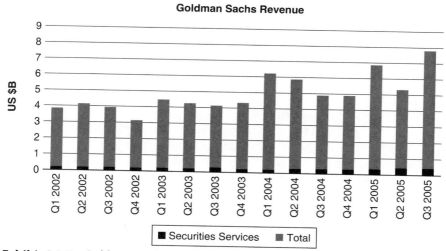

Exhibit 14.5 Goldman Sachs revenues 2002–2005. *Source:* Aite Group.

---

[4] Sang Lee, "Shaking Up Prime Brokerage: Unbundling Securities Lending, Financing, and Derivatives Transactions," Aite Group Report 200510171 (October 2005): 12–14.

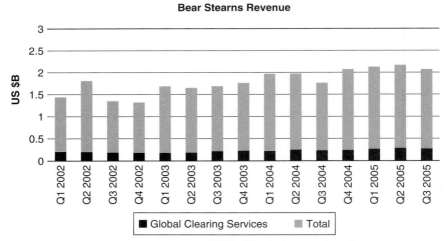

Exhibit 14.6 Bear Stearns revenues 2002–2005. *Source:* Aite Group.

advantage of one prime broker versus another is the ability to provide a broad product range of services efficiently in different asset classes. It is clear that prime brokerage can benefit greatly from new technological enhancements such as trade automation and straight-through processing (STP). Hedge funds can appreciate real-time reporting when a trade is entered into a system and routed to another instantaneously. The benefits of this will be a reduction in settlement time from T+3 to same trade date or T+1. This can minimize unsettled position risk, providing less exposure to volatile markets and settlement default. It can also eliminate manual intervention in the back office, ensure automated trade affirmation, and reduce operational costs. It is important for a prime broker to have strong technological capabilities. The broker should be able to offer a variety of proprietary applications, including portfolio reporting and transparency reporting for the hedge fund clients. One of the dangers is the fact that some prime brokers operate as subunits of trading divisions. When a prime broker does not operate as a distinct and separate entity, confidentiality of trading activity of different positions will be compromised. A frugal move for hedge funds would be to disperse their trading activity spread out among different prime brokers to minimize the ability of a prime broker to use your information to their benefit.

Chapter 15

Profiling the Leading Vendors

15.1 Introduction

Institutions have been driven toward algorithmic trading, a computerized strategy that slices large orders into smaller pieces to avoid market impact. The strategy has greater potential for reducing transaction costs and measuring returns against a chosen benchmark. According to Larry Tabb of the TABB Group, algorithmic trading is composed of six components. The first is high-speed market data, which is the platform that everything else depends on. The next component is the decision as to what assets to buy or sell to achieve driving quantitative strategies in their investment process. The decision comes out of computers that have been programmed to look for measures within the market data and trading. The third component is trade execution, which determines what algorithm should be used to actually carry out the trade. From there the way the order is routed is determined. Many firms have developed smart order-routing systems that use a set of rules to automate the search for best price. The fifth component is the actual matching process. Traditionally that was straightforward; the order went to an exchange or Electronic Communication Network (ECN), but now there is a lot of internalization, so there's variability in that model. The last step is transaction cost analysis, which looks at the trading model and the execution to see how well the trading process worked.[1] The basic building blocks of algorithmic trading are designed to capture real-time trading opportunities,

---

[1] "Algorithmic Trading: 4 Perspectives," *Futures Industry*, July–August 2005, http://www. futuresindustry.org/fimagazi-1929.asp?a=1052&iss=154.

identifying tiny market inefficiencies relating to various factors such as price, volume, liquidity, benchmarks, and so on. Exhibit 15.1 illustates the elements of algorithmic trading.

According to the Aite Group, the demand for algorithmic trading services continues to increase. At the end of 2004, over US $200 million was spent on different IT components that make up algorithmic trading services. IT spending on Order Management Systems (OMSs) accounted for over 60% of total spending in 2004. The Aite Group expects independent technology providers to become more active with vendors and be in the position to use multiple distribution channels to capture additional market shares. Eric Goldberg, co-founder of Portware, a vendor of algorithmic trading systems applicable to equity, futures, and for-exchange markets, states that one of the key factors that determines how quickly algorithmic trading spreads is the adoption of a standard communication protocol. When everyone has a different protocol, the cost to translate all those protocols really limits access for the typical trader. One of the reasons why algorithmic trading is so advanced in equities is that marketplace very quickly standardized with the FIX protocol. Now standardized protocols are coming into place in many different asset classes and that barrier to access is really coming down.

Technology providers who are focused on algorithmic trading face increasing competition with one another as well as with brokers using proprietary trading platforms (see Exhibit 15.2). Technology providers can also simultaneously serve the sell and buy side but also provide cross-asset capability on one platform. Algorithmic trading technology providers also face competition from technology providers such as OMS vendors who currently

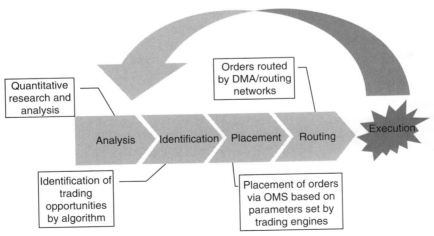

Exhibit 15.1   *Source:* Aite Group.

function as facilitators and gatekeepers to various financial institutions. A new generation of OMSs that provide automated trading and integrated portfolio suites with improved trade functionality is increasing the number of affordable options available on the market. Firms such as New York based– Advanced Financial Applications Impact Pro offer a basic trade blotter with execution capability. Firms such as Reuters and Bloomberg are offering trade counterparty connectivity services, which also include algorithmic trading. A new wave of applications that provide full trading suites, such as portfolio modeling, trade blotter, and pre- and post-trade compliance, are being offered by firms such as Tradeware, Portware, Bloomberg, Reuters, and European-based vendors such as Trading Screen. These products, which were once expensive to implement and maintain, are now becoming accessible to new entrants due to price pressure, for example, hedge funds and smaller invest-ment management firms. Portware and FlexTrade are focusing on hedge funds with solutions that allow users to customize quantitative trading strat-egies alongside traditional risk arbitrage and long/short strategies. As the market for high-priced custom implementation becomes saturated, vendors will shift their focus to midtier asset managers where once only the largest financial firms could justify the expense. More players will implement elec-tronic access to markets integrating trading and portfolio management suites. Total market spending for trading systems was $445 million in 2004, and potentially can reach $701 million in 2007 according to Celent.[2]

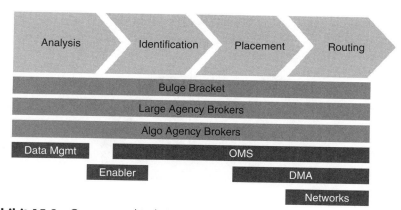

Exhibit 15.2 Competitive landscape. *Source:* Aite Group.

---

[2] Denise Valentine, "OMS: Breaking Down Barriers," *Wall Street & Technology*, August 22, 2005.

15.2 Profiling Leading Vendors

The source of the profiles that follow is *Algorithmic Trading Technology*, Aite Group, April 2005.

VHAYU TECHNOLOGIES

Vhayu Technologies is a leading provider of a real-time software platform that enables financial institutions to capture, store, and analyze enormous amounts of historical data. Vhayu's platform, called "Velocity," has been used widely for tick data management to allow clients to perform real-time trading analysis. Velocity was designed to be scalable and cost effective and was built on a Windows platform. The Velocity platform can communicate with other internal and external systems via FIX, TC/IP, RMDS, and TIB. The platform has the ability to process thousands of streams of real-time data in its raw data format without filtering. The platform has the ability to enable real-time trade decision making. Clients can perform dynamic VWAP analysis based on customizable intervals and trading durations (see Exhibit 15.3). Vhayu's data store captures and stores streaming and historical data in a central location, which supports equities, FX, futures, and fixed income. It has the ability to interface with statistical packages such as Excel, MATLAB, and S-PLUS.

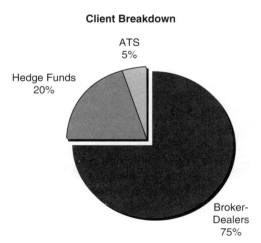

Client Breakdown

ATS
5%

Hedge Funds
20%

Broker-
Dealers
75%

Exhibit 15.3 Client breakdown of Vhayu. *Source:* Vhayu Technologies, Aite Group.

XENOMORPH

Xenomorph is a leading player in the high-performance data management market. Xenomorph began building a data management platform, based on historical time-series market data, designed to enable users to perform comprehensive correlation and volatility analysis on baskets of assets. Xenomorph's core data management platform is TimeScape, which is an object-relational database called Xenomorph XDB. It was designed to handle massive amounts of data in order to facilitate the rapid analysis of trade opportunities and risk management. The Xenomorph XDB provides higher performance than traditional relational databases currently on the market. This database has the ability to handle all major asset classes including equities, fixed income, and derivatives. It performs integrated analysis of historical time-series and real-time tick data. It can take business logic and transport that calculation to the centralized database. It has a flexible data model to handle multiple instrument data feeds in a consistent manner and rapidly support any new products that can be integrated into existing legacy systems and traditional relational databases using TimeScape XDK. This product can also be fully compatible with XML Web services based on SOAP and .NET.

Xenomorph begins its second decade of growth. Xenomorph's Time-Scape is the current product enhanced and refined over the last 10 years. They currently have 30 clients globally, with investment banks accounting for 50% of their client base, and hedge funds specializing in convertible bond and statistical arbitrage along with asset management firms comprising the remainder.

APAMA

Apama is an independent financial technology firm, founded in 2000, which provides outsourced trading strategies. Apama is designed to reduce the time taken to deploy and maintain an algorithmic trading solution. Apama currently has clients on both the buy and the sell side, with major clients including JP Morgan, ABN Amro, and Deutsche Bank. They are headquartered in Cambridge, England. Apama enables traders to make efficient trading decisions without spending substantial resources developing an in-house algorithmic trading strategy. It can continuously monitor, adjust, and implement trading strategies in real time. Apama's solution consists of an algorithmic trading engine called "Event Manager," market data connections called "Adapters," and trading strategy modeling/deployment tools called "Event Modeler."

- **Apama Event Manager** represents the core of the Apama platform. Trade decisions can be made in real time, because it provides its users with the ability to filter numerous data streams such as exchange feeds, news feeds, proprietary data, and reference data detecting various patterns of events in subseconds. The Event Manager acts as a filter sifting through data streams in real time.
- **Apama Event Modeler** functions as a blank canvas where clients can create trading strategies from scratch or use various building blocks provided by Apama. Traders can use dashboards to create and manage instances of trading strategies.
- **Integration Adapter Framework (IAF)** is a framework that enables seamless integration with databases, middleware, and other internal as well as external systems.

FLEXTRADE

FlexTrade is one of the leading broker-neutral, trade order management providers in the algorithmic trading market. Their leading product, Flex-TRADER, challenged the once-dominant QuantEX marketed by ITG. FlexTRADER is built in C++, providing clients the ability to utilize existing algorithms or creating their own. Key features and functionality of Flex-TRADER include the following:

1. FlexTRADER supports CMS for NYSE securities and FIX for other execution venues.
2. FlexTRADER handles multiple asset classes including global equities, FX, futures, and single stock futures, etc.
3. FlexTrade provides prepackaged algorithms such as Risk Arb, Long/Short, and VWAP, etc.
4. Clients can modify prepackaged algorithms and/or create new ones using the platform.
5. Traders can rapidly modify their trading strategies intraday reacting to real-time market conditions.
6. Direct market runs on access to all major sources of liquidity.
7. FlexTRADER enables traders to handle both single stock and portfolio trading.
8. FlexTRADER runs on Sun Solaris, Linux, and Windows NT.

Other FlexTrade products include the following:

- **FlexTQM**   Post-trade transaction cost analysis tool.
- **FlexDMA**   Provides a real-time, aggregated view of the market and enables rapid routing to appropriate liquidity sources.

- **FlexSIMULATOR**   Enables clients to build and test trading strategies using real-time and historical tick data.
- **eFlexTRADER**   Hosted version of FlexTRADER accessible via the Internet. Sell-side firms can market this product to their own clients to attract additional order flow.

PORTWARE

Portware is a leading provider of buy-side and sell-side trade and execution management software for basket, single-asset and automated quantitative trading. Portware Professional, its core product, is a centralized platform for trade and execution management. Portware was founded in 2000 and is headquartered in New York, with an office in London.

Portware Professional is an order management system, capable of handling both single-asset and portfolio/basket trading with multiuser support. Some of the key features and functionality of Portware Professional include the following:

1. The platform is built on Java and can handle all major financial products including equities, futures, options, fixed income, and FX.
2. Portware easily integrates into existing workflow via FIX, Java, and Socket APIs.
3. Portware offers prepackaged algorithms (VWAP, Pairs, Long/Short, etc.) but also enables customization and the ability to connect to broker-provided algorithms.
4. Clients can use Portware Professional to develop their own algorithms.
5. Portware can be used as a completely independent platform.
6. Portware fully facilitates portfolio, basket, and index trading. Clients can import lists from any application, sort lists, conduct pre- and post-trade analysis, and modify basket strategies.
7. A robust transaction-cost-analysis feature is integrated into Portware Professional. Clients can compare execution performance by model, broker, destination, sector, and more against predefined benchmarks in real-time monitor slippage.
8. Portware provides comprehensive position management capability with consolidated real-time view of market data, actionable alerts and risk management, and intraday maintenance of positions for all clients, accounts, and strategies.
9. Portware provides automated reporting capability for best execution practices, OATS, ACT, and trade reports against multiple benchmarks.

10. Portware provides extensive connectivity to networks and OMS.
11. Portware supports all market data feeds including proprietary data.

QUANT HOUSE

Quant House is the next generation company offering end-to-end program trading solutions to trade ahead. Ultralow latency market data technologies, trading strategies development framework, execution engine and infrastructures services enable Quant House to deliver end-to-end performance for your program trading business.

Main Focus

- Ultralow latency market data technologies
- Program trading strategies development framework
- Execution engine
- Infrastructure services
- Professional customer support

Shareholders

Quant House has the benefit and support of a very experienced group of investors. The Investor group is led by one of the world's largest global brokerage organizations, Fimat International Banque, subsidiary of "Société Générale Group."

QUANTITATIVE SERVICES GROUP

Quantitative Services Group (QSG) is an independent research consulting company that provides analytical stock selection research and transaction cost analysis. QSG's core products in the algorithmic trading markets are T-Cost Pro and Factor Analyst. QSG is headquartered in Naperville, Ilinois.
QSG currently provides three major services for their clients:

- **Factor analyst**   This stock selection research service leverages over 300 different stock selection indicators maintained and updated for portfolio construction and stock selection.
- **Virtual research analyst**   Portfolio managers can use this service to support any disciplined stock selection strategy. This research enables customization of candidate identification criteria, quick screening, backtesting, and quality control.

- **T-Cost Pro** A Web-based transaction cost management product capable of producing detailed analysis of time-stamped executions on a T+1 basis.

QSG products are designed to help buy-side firms overcome the mediocrity associated with using simple benchmarks such as VWAP to conduct transaction cost analysis. QSG is currently in an ideal position to provide TCA service to buy-side firms and is also working on developing pre-trade analytics to provide additional structure to a growing algorithmic trading market.

LAVA TRADING

Lava Trading is a leading trading technology provider for the equities and foreign exchange markets. Lava pioneered the institutional DMA market, with more than 20 investment banks in the United States as its clients. Lava was acquired by Citigroup in July 2004 and has made significant progress gaining traction in the buy-side market, having signed up more than 40% of the top 50 asset management firms and hedge funds. Lava Trading also accounts for more than 10% of total ETF trading volume in addition to a 15% OTC market share and rapid adoption in the electronic listed trading arena. Lava Trading is headquartered in New York with offices in San Francisco and London.

Lava has become a leading front-office trading platform provider, with offerings in equities order management side, as well as in foreign exchange.

Lava's leading products include the following six programs:

ColorBook Lava's patented technology, ColorBook, aggregates real-time depth of book data from all major liquidity destinations. It provides intelligent order routing and high speed liquidity access.

DarkBook A component of ColorBook, which enables traders to access hidden reserves at various liquidity pools, using smart tools to access larger pools of liquidity.

LavaPI A component of ColorBook, which enables traders to capture price improvement, a major differentiator in best execution quality.

ColorPalette An institutional-strength order management system, ColorPalette has become the first choice among the largest broker-dealers in the United States.

ColorData ColorData provides real-time, consolidated market data from all major liquidity sources. ColorData Archive allows users to download and save historical data from the previous six months for analytics and compliance purposes.

LavaFX LavaFX leverages the technical infrastructure of Lava Trading to deliver aggregated FX liquidity destinations through a single access point. Liquidity providers to the LavaFX platform include ABN Amro,

Barclays Capital, Citibank, Deutsche Bank, Dresdner Kleinwort Wasserstein, HSBC, and Royal Bank of Scotland among others.

NEOVEST, INC

Neovest, Inc is an independent trading software provider to the buy side, focusing especially on the hedge fund market. It was founded in November 1999, as part of Neovest Holdings, part of the merged entities of Roberts-Slade Inc (RSI), an investment software firm, and The Volume Investor, Inc (TVI), an institutional broker-dealer providing equity research.

Neovest's current trade management system includes the following features:

1. Direct market access to all of the major liquidity destinations
2. Links to and support for full functionality of the leading algorithmic trading engines provided by BoA Securities, Credit Suisse, Deutsche Bank, JP Morgan, Lehman Brothers, Merrill Lynch, and UBS, etc.
3. Connectivity to leading broker and crossing networks
4. Robust analytics tools including filtering/reverse filtering, advanced charting (tick, intraday, daily, weekly, or monthly quotes)
5. Advanced order entry options, including basket/list trading, role-based trading, order slicing, conditional orders, etc.
6. Support for trade executions of equities, futures, options, and FX

Neovest provides a single-window view into major trading venues and partners, through its extensive connectivity to leading broker networks, clearing firms, and major order management systems to enable its clients to easily access all of the major counterparties and liquidity destinations.

SUNGARD TRADING SYSTEMS

SunGard has dominated the OTC equities order management system market with its product called BRASS. SunGard systems account for over 70% of NASDAQ trades. SunGard has also been capturing market share in the algorithmic trading market. BRASS has over 170 clients, representing one of the leading sell-side OMSs in the United States. SunGard offers algorithmic trading through BRASS, UMA, and soon Broker Direct U2, a broker-sponsored version of the new DMA system. Broker Direct U2 has become SunGard's leading DMA platform. Broker Direct U2 includes the following key features and functionality:

1. Full integration with BRASS.
2. FIX API enables clients to link their OMS, front-office GUI, program trading systems, and proprietary trading engines.

3. The ViewTrader feature allows centralized management of trading among groups of traders, enabling a team of traders to efficiently manage trading of multiple securities using the same set of orders and positions.
4. Configurable drop-copy functionality enables firms to attach trader and book-of-business data to drop copies, so that a particular trade execution can be segregated to a specific book-of-business.
5. The Advanced Smart Agents feature allows traders to seek best execution with order-based, volume-based, time-effective, randomization agents and time-slicing agents.

SunGard has been a dominant force in the U.S. equities trading market for decades. SunGard is looking to develop new products and services in addition to leveraging its BRASS platform to capture additional clients.

RADIANZ

Radianz is the largest IP network supporting the financial services industry. It was founded in 2000 as a partnership between Reuters and Equant, which Reuters eventually bought out. Radianz is exclusively focused on the financial services industry, with a particular emphasis on enabling access to pre-trade and post-trade applications and services. Some of the key features of Radianz include the following:

1. RadianzNet is the largest secure IP network in the financial services industry with over 11,000 endpoints.
2. RadianzNet has 130 companies with services on the network with 370 available applications, averaging 2.7 applications per financial institution.
3. With 1,000 unique endpoints, RadianzNet is the largest FIX community in the world.

TRANSACTION NETWORK SERVICES, INC.

TNS was founded in 1990 and currently has four business divisions that provide services globally (see Exhibit 15.4):

1. Point-of-Sales (POS) Services
2. Telecommunications
3. Financial Services
4. International Services

TNS has launched its secure trading extranet, which is designed to facilitate the exchange of data and transactions. It provides end-to-end

Revenue Breakdown

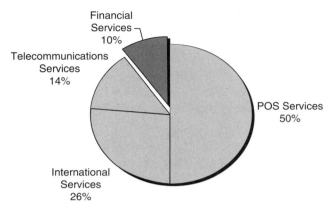

Total Revenue as of June 30, 2004 = US $238.8 Million

Exhibit 15.4   Four business divisions within TNS. *Source:* TNS.

encryption for all FIX-based messages and allows connectivity with all FIX-enabled trading platforms. These are some of the key features of the secure trading extranet:

- Over 900 leveraged endpoints on the network, including most of the major liquidity destinations, brokers, industry utilities, broker desks, etc.
- Use of Points-of-Presence (POPs) and access validation, among others, to provide security over the network.
- All network components are managed 365 days a year.
- Redundant POPs, alternate carriers, and backup power systems to ensure reliability and uptime.

TNS has increased its adoption rate of algorithmic trading. Some of TNS's recent initiatives within the algorithmic trading market include

- leveraging the existing network infrastructure to provide simple and quick connectivity with minimum latency;
- working closely with leading OMS providers and the sell-side to facilitate trading activities as well as support analytical products on the network;
- positioning itself as a one-stop-shop to all major trading partners, exchanges, market data, and DMA;
- carrying raw data directly from major exchanges and ECNs, instead of via data consolidators to eliminate data latency;

- working with firms with proprietary systems to increase endpoints;
- generating additional business for TNS as it becomes the connectivity specialist for private label deals.

TNS has made an enormous amount of progress in the financial services market by focusing on supporting mission-critical operations through its growing network.

SunGard Transaction Network

SunGard Transaction Network (STN) is a trading network that enables clients to automate and manage the full life cycle of a trade, including post-trade processing. Provided by the SunGard Financial Networks Group within SunGard, STN features connectivity to over 1,200 buy-side clients and 175 broker-dealers in its equities capital markets area.

STN produces three different products:

1. **STN Funds** Facilitates mutual fund transactions, providing services to employee benefit plans and administrators, asset managers, and bank/trust firms.
2. **STN Money Markets** Facilitates transactions of short-term investment vehicles such as commercial paper, CDs, time deposits, and money market funds to corporate treasurers, asset managers, and mutual fund companies.
3. **STN Securities** Facilitates communications between buy-side firms and their brokers and custodians by utilizing open protocols, and supports full life cycle of trades for equities and fixed-income products.

STN Securities is the core product for SunGard Financial Network in the algorithmic trading services market. STN currently has Passport, and SunGard's BRASS and Broker Direct U2.

15.3 Order Management Systems

The source for information provided in this section is Capital Institutional Services, Inc. Fourth Quarter 2005.

Advent Moxy

Moxy (see www.advent.com) is licensed by bank trust departments, money managers, broker-dealers, wrap sponsors, financial planners, hedge funds, mutual funds, corporations, family offices, and insurance companies.

The range of assets under management is from $100 million to over $40 billion, with the typical client having between $3 to $5 billion in assets under management. Moxy is currently licensed at over 630 firms and has a presence in the United States, Europe, Canada, Mexico, Australia, and the Far East. Moxy runs on Microsoft SQL Server 2000. The system requires Windows NT or Windows 2000 on the server and Windows NT or Windows 2000 on the workstation.

Advent Software, Inc. is a provider of Enterprise Investment Management solutions, offering stand-alone and client/server software products, data interfaces, and related services that automate and integrate mission-critical functions of investment management organizations. Advent has licensed its products to more than 6,000 financial institutions in 36 countries for use by more than 60,000 concurrent users. The company's common stock is traded on the NASDAQ National Market under the symbol ADVS.

ANTARES

Antares (see www.ssctech.com) is marketed and sold to buy-side money managers including hedge funds, family offices, institutional asset managers, proprietary trading desks, short-term (money market) desks, pension funds, and mutual funds. The range of assets under management for an Antares client is from $100 million for some of the smaller hedge funds, and up to $75 billion for the larger asset managers. The typical Antares client has $1 to $10 billion in assets under management. Antares has an open database client/server (Sybase or Microsoft SQL Server) architecture, which runs on the Windows Server operating system and/or Solaris UNIX.

SS&C Technologies, based out of Windsor, Connecticut with offices in the United States, Canada, Europe, and Asia, is a provider of financial software solutions, services, and expertise to asset managers worldwide. SS&C primarily targets its products and services to large-scale, sophisticated investment enterprises that use the trading, accounting, reporting, and analysis solutions.

BLOOMBERG PORTFOLIO ORDER MANAGEMENT SYSTEM

The Bloomberg Portfolio Order Management System (see www.bloom berg.com) is used by money managers, investment advisors, pension funds, mutual funds, state agencies, bank trust departments, and insurance companies. Bloomberg POMS is employed by both fixed-income and equity clients and has global product coverage. Currently POMS is employed at over 250 buy-side firms globally. The range of assets under management is from $500 million to $500 billion, with the typical POMS client having between $5 to $50 billion in assets under management. Bloomberg POMS customers have their own secure encrypted database housing account and position data. The databases are proprietarily built and maintained by Bloomberg. The Bloomberg POMS applications run on the same platform as the Bloomberg Professional Service and are provided in an ASP model. Real-time and batch trade, Security Master, and customizable data feeds are sent via TCP/IP and FTP.

Bloomberg L.P. was founded in 1981. It provides news, pricing, and analytics via the Bloomberg Professional Service to over 162,000 dedicated desktop terminals globally. Bloomberg POMS is a suite of front-end trade order management applications offered over the Bloomberg Professional Service.

CHARLES RIVER TRADING SYSTEM

The Charles River Investment Management System (Charles River IMS/ see www.crd.com) is a comprehensive, integrated, front- and middle-office suite for all security types. Each of the suite's three components is available as a stand-alone application: Charles River Manager offers sophisticated tools for portfolio management including "what if" analysis, tax impact management, P&L analysis, modeling, portfolio rebalancing, and order generation. Charles River Trader provides order management, auto-routing capabilities, strategy-based trading, electronic order placement (including Charles River certified FIX network), and liquidity access. Charles River Compliance offers global, real-time, pre-trade, post-execution, and port-folio-level compliance monitoring. Charles River Manager, Charles River Trader, and Charles River Compliance offer an enterprise solution on one integrated platform. Deploy the full suite (Charles River IMS) or integrate individual components with existing systems.

DECALOG

Decalog (see www.sungard.com) is a leading trading and portfolio manage-ment system for the buy-side investment management industry. Decalog helps reduce the operational and integration costs and also increases efficiency. It provides order management, decision support, and pre- and post-trade compliance control through a modular suite. The main modules are Decalog Trader, Decalog Compliance, and Decalog Manager. Decalog is designed to integrate with external or internal systems. Decalog is licensed by global asset management organizations, including institutional investment managers, mutual funds, insurance companies, and hedge funds. Client assets range from $8 billion to over $300 billion with the typical client having $50 billion under management.

EZE CASTLE TRADERS CONSOLE

Traders Console (see www.ezecastlesoftware.com) features an N-tier messaging, service-based architecture. This architecture enables Traders Console (TC) to be a truly scalable, real-time solution. TC's application services are designed to run on Windows Server 2000 and 2003; the database server on Microsoft SQL Server 2000. The client workstation is certified on Windows 2000 and XP. Client assets under management range from $150 million to over $450 billion. Eze Castle has over 220 clients utilizing Traders Console with typical clients being investment advisors and hedge funds. Founded in 1995, Eze Castle Software, Inc. is a software company providing products to the investment management market. With a rapidly growing client list and offices in Boston, New York, San Francisco, Stamford, and London, Eze Castle Software is one of the largest trade order management firms in the financial services industry and has approximately 140 employees worldwide.

INDATA

Precision Trading, INDATA's (see www.indataweb.com) "best of breed" trade order management system, links traders with portfolio managers, executing brokers, and back-office staff in real time, resulting in paperless trading. Open/relational database (Microsoft SQL Server 2000) client/server architecture runs on Windows XP/2000. Client PCs utilize Windows XP/2000. Browser-based platform via InContact.net. SQL Server Microsoft Reporting Services allows browser-based delivery of information. The range of assets under management is from $400 million to over $100 billion. The typical client is a buy-side asset management firm with a blend of institutional, taxable accounts, mutual funds, and hedge funds.

LATENTZERO

Capstone is LatentZero's (see www.latentzero.com) complete front-office product for asset management companies. The individual components of Capstone can also be implemented separately or as part of a "best of breed" approach. Capstone offers clients the full benefits of LatentZero's scalable, future-proof technology, high-speed implementation, and commitment to product development. LatentZero's products can be easily integrated as part of the client's overall STP solution. LatentZero's products are designed to fully support all instrument types (equity, debt, money market, mutual funds, derivatives, and currency). Clients license anywhere from 10 users to over 100 and typically trade on average 250,000 shares per day. Typical clients are institutional asset managers or fund managers who manage a diverse set of holdings including equities, fixed income, and derivatives.

LongView

LongView Trading is Linedata's (see www.linedata.com) powerful, electronic, global, multiasset class Order Management System (OMS) developed to support the needs of portfolio managers, traders, compliance officers, and operations personnel. The comprehensive system provides portfolio modeling, electronic trading, pre-trade compliance, and unparalleled access to liquidity. Through numerous partnerships and seamless integration. LongView Trading offers customers access to the liquidity sources of their choice. Linedata Services is the innovative leader in the financial technology market, delivering "best of breed" global solutions and consulting services for asset management, leasing and credit finance, and employee savings. Linedata's asset management offerings include a full array of front-, middle-, and back-office products designed to help streamline the investment process. Linedata Services is committed to innovation and investment in continuous technology to meet the growing needs of sophisticated global investors.

MacGregor XIP 7s

MacGregor XIP 7s represents Macgregor's (see www.macgregor.com) third generation of order management technology and a new class of solution for asset managers. Unlike traditional Order Management Systems (OMSs) that optimize functional silos and end at the walls of the firm, XIP 7s optimizes the execution process from initial portfolio decision to final settlement by connecting all internal and external parties involved. This unique networked platform is the industry's first Order Management Network (OMN) and is capable of helping firms reduce errors, improve efficiencies, and achieve best execution. MacGregor has over 100 buy-side clients and over 275 sell-side clients and other service providers collaborating on the MacGregor XIP 7 OMN.

Appendix: The Implementation of Trading Systems

A.1 Overview

Front-office trading systems constitute the backbone of the technical infrastructure, which supports traders by processing their executions. The adoption of electronic trading systems has transformed the landscape of trading venues, forcing a change in market architecture and trading possibilities. Electronic trading removes geographical restraints and allows for continuous interaction. New trading systems are designed to feature linkage to electronic order routing and the dissemination of trade information and may link through to clearing and settlements. Existing market structures, regulatory and competitive factors, and the varied needs of traders have all affected the integration of new technology into mainstream trading. A trading system is usually linked to many applications both inside and outside of the organization. Seamless integration from front to back through straight-through processing requires well-designed workflows. Electronic trading can make markets more contestable, allowing participants to enter more cheaply and enabling greater linkage to a variety of products. Electronic systems can link together sources of liquidity and harness efficiencies that contribute to consolidation. The basic role of a trading system is to

1. capture deals of a trading desk or department;
2. allow traders to keep track of their position, both in terms of absolute numbers as well as derived numbers, i.e., P&L;

3. allow risk management to monitor the risk of a desk or department, usually yielding a breakdown of risk numbers to different asset classes, risk types, or locations;
4. assure compliance of the trading operation with regulatory or internal rules and market conformity;
5. connect various back-office and accounting systems.

A new trading system can be implemented either through scratch or replacing one or more existing systems. Many organizations have chosen to consolidate their existing front-office system due to cost pressure, often ending up with a single system covering all asset classes. When a new trading system is designed, an implementation project must be organized.

A.2 Project Phases

PHASE 1—ANALYZE

- Identify financial instruments, workflows, and trade life cycle of system
- Organize a high-level system architecture that includes all interfaces to be built by the project
- Organize plan for data migration and testing to be carried out
- Develop project plan for design and build phase

PHASE 2—DESIGN

- Organization of structure and user access rights
- Portfolio/book structure
- Instrument capture
- Static data, counterparty details, settlement instructions
- Specification of workflow and trade cycle events
- Modeling of interest rate curves, spread curves
- Specification of P&L and risk measures

PHASE 3—BUILD

- Building of reports, interfaces, and data migration tools
- Implementation of technical architecture, in particular setup of production and test servers
- Preparation of test phase
- User training
- Data migration testing
- System test

- Integration test
- User acceptance test
- Roll-out
- Final data migration

A.2 User Acceptance Testing

Many trading systems are used to manage positions in the billions and to transfer large amounts of money. Extensive testing is required with proper up-front planning and preparation both on a high level in the form of a testing strategy and on a detailed level in the form of test cases. The following are the different types of testing that an implementation project should be considering:

1. **Developer test**   Tests on the level of individual software functions or modules, carried out by developers; sometimes called unit tests. These tests are rarely properly documented and it is often difficult for project management to assess the module.
2. **Model test**   Intensive test of all mathematical models implemented by the trading system, which include valuation and financial quantities.
3. **System test**   Once all modules are finished and the trading system is properly implemented, all workflows as well as reports of the system should be tested prior to hooking it up to other systems. The main objective is to verify whether the user rights structure supports the workflows designed by the project team.
4. **Integration test**   The intention of this test is to verify that the cross-system workflows and data flows are functioning properly and to start testing the interfaces to these systems both individually and collectively.
5. **Data migration test**   Data migration can be one of the most complex tasks in a trading system implementation. The initial upload of instrument static and trade data can often prove difficult. False instrument or trade data can have negative consequences.
6. **User acceptance test (UAT)**   In a UAT case, future users of the trading system will ultimately decide whether or not the implementation will be a success. Cases are often provided for future use of the system.
7. **Parallel phase**   In highly critical environments, a parallel run where trades are entered into both old and new systems in parallel can be a solution in giving users the confidence that the new system will fully support operations. Another critical point is to what extent downstream systems can be run parallel.

A.3 From Implementation to Customization

Implementing trading systems can require a considerable amount of customization, time, and resources. In any system implementation, it is important to prioritize from the beginning and be able to distinguish between critical and less critical issues. Vendors providing software for customers to use for trading often offer complex systems, which allow for a high degree of customization. However, many customers believe an out-of-the-box functionality should be sufficient in supporting their current workflows, and only need to link connectivity to interface with a couple of other systems. Prioritization from a develop phase often rarely coincides with the priorities of the future users, so customizing a new trading system may take a considerable amount of time, often exceeding one year once implementation starts.

A.4 The Challenges of Data Integration

One of the most critical project tasks in implementing a new trading platform is usually data integration. Without the required static data uploaded daily or at the very least with subsequent manual maintenance, no deal can be properly priced, or captured in a system, or worse yet, the instrument is missing altogether. If the deal cannot be forwarded to a downstream system or matched with the counterparty, the settlement will most likely fail. Building such interfaces with the proper static data is often a manually intensive, tedious, and lengthy process. Any critical task next to data integration is basic parameterization of the system. This comprises mainly the specification of how various data items, instruments, and counterparties will be mapped to the data model of the trading platform. One of the biggest challenges surrounding parameterization is the difficulty in modifying the interface once the systems have moved to production. Data migration is a highly critical task in implementing a new trading platform, It is not sufficient to just identify source systems for the required data, and to write the upload scripts. Data quality, data cleansing, and how the uploaded data is reconciled must also be addressed.

A.5 Supporting Financial Products

Most trading systems will not offer the latest models, often missing support for some financial products. Software suppliers are often missing the capacity to incorporate every product into their system and only implement them when sufficient demand arises. This frequently poses problems for organizations with an active business in such areas. They often end up either managing these products outside the trading systems or integrating their in-house models with the trading system. Frequently, in-house models are slow and hardly suitable for real-time regulatory reporting.

Implementing a new trading system is a challenging task, which often requires a longer time frame than initially anticipated.

Glossary of Terms

A

Access Rule sets forth new standards governing access to quotations in NMS stocks. First, it enables the use of private linkages offered by a variety of connectivity providers. The lower cost and increased flexibility of connectivity in recent years have made private linkages a feasible alternative to hard linkages. Market participants may obtain indirect access to quotations displayed by a particular trading center through the members, subscribers, or customers of that trading center.

agency brokers either provide direct access services, and/or algorithmic trading services. Most of these firms are focused on supporting algorithmic trading as an efficient means to offer their traditional agency brokerage services. The most established agency brokers include BNY brokerage, Instinet, and ITG. Smaller agency brokers include Automated Trading Desk (ATD), Miletus Trading, Lime Brokerage, FutureTrade, UNX, and EdgeTrade.

algorithmic trading defined as "placing a buy or sell order of a defined quantity into a quantitative model that automatically generates the timing of orders and the size of orders based on goals specified by the parameters and constraints of the algorithm."[1] The term is imprecise and ambiguous. Any trader following a set protocol could be said to have an algorithmic strategy.

---

[1] The TowerGroup, s.v. "Algorithmic Trading," *Glossary of Terms*, http://www.towergroup. com/research/content/glossary.jsp?page=1&glossaryId=382.

arrival price   the price of a stock at the time the order is raised and used as a pre-trade benchmark to measure execution quality. The difference between the order arrival price and the execution price can be used to determine the implementation shortfall.

auction systems   enable participants to conduct electronic auctions of securities offerings. Some auction systems are tailored to new issues in the primary market. Others focus on auctions of secondary market offerings by investors or others. In either case, a seller or issuer typically posts the details of a security being offered for sale and the specific terms of the auction, whether the auction is single price or multiple price, the time the auction is open, whether partial orders will be filled, etc. Buyers can submit bids for the offered securities, and the offering is awarded to the bidder who offers the highest price or lowest yield. In some cases, the identities of the bidders and the amounts of the bids are kept anonymous.

automated trading   trades in which prices can be published and executed by a computer.

B

bid-ask spread or implicit cost   the price at which an investor or money manager can purchase an asset (the dealer's ask price) and the price at which you can sell the same asset at the same point in time (the dealer's bid price). The price impact this usually creates by trading an asset pushes up the price when buying an asset and pushes it down while selling.

black box   a terminology for any system that takes orders and breaks them down into smaller ones. Black box trading tends to mean trades executed by a computer that has taken in certain market data and decides which stocks to buy or sell, and typically when and how much.

C

circuit breakers   determine whether or not trading will be halted temporarily or stopped entirely. The securities and futures markets have circuit breakers that provide for brief, coordinated cross-market trading halts during a severe market decline as measured by a single-day decrease in the Dow Jones Industrial Average (DJIA).

Consolidated Tape Association (CTA)   Consolidated Tape Association (CTA) oversees the dissemination of real-time trade and quote information in New York Stock Exchange and American Stock Exchange listed securities. (Technically, there are two Plans, the Consolidated Tape Plan, which governs trades and the Consolidated Quotation Plan, which governs quotes.) Since the late 1970s, all SEC-registered exchanges and market centers that trade NYSE- or AMEX-listed securities send their trades and quotes to a central consolidator where the Consolidated Tape System (CTS) and Consolidated Quote System (CQS) data streams are produced and distributed worldwide.

continuous crossing   provides access to liquidity and negotiations throughout the day. It provides more information than the scheduled crossing model and is prone to information leakage.

cross-matching systems   generally bring both dealers and institutional investors together in electronic trading networks that provide real-time or periodic cross-matching sessions. Customers are able to enter anonymous buy and sell orders with multiple counterparties and can automatically execute these prices at the same posted prices as other "hit" or "lifted" trades. In some cases, customers are able to initiate negotiation sessions to establish the terms of trades.

D

dark box model   a hybrid between the continuous and scheduled models. This allows firms to hide liquidity in the dark box, providing price improvement to both sides without the broadcast of any information.

Decimalization   mandate that forced market makers and buy-side institutions to switch from valuing stocks in traditional sixteenths ($.0625) to valuing them in penny spreads ($.01), which increased price points from 6 for every dollar to 100.

Depository Trust & Clearing Corporation (DTCC)   Depository Trust & Clearing Corporation (DTCC), through its subsidiaries, provides clearance, settlement, and information services for equities, corporate and municipal bonds, government and mortgage-backed securities, and over-the-counter credit derivatives. DTCC's depository also provides custody and asset servicing for more than two million securities issues from the United States and 100 other countries and territories. In addition, DTCC is a leading processor of mutual funds and insurance transactions, linking funds and carriers with their distribution networks. DTCC has operating facilities in multiple locations in the United States and overseas.

direct market access (DMA)   offers investors a direct and efficient method of accessing electronic exchanges through Internet trading. DMA gives the individual an autonomous role in deciding on an investment strategy matching buyers and sellers directly. This trading methodology allows investors to execute orders through specific destinations such as market makers, exchanges, and Electronic Communication Networks (ECNs). Some trading may continue to rely on personal contacts, which can be enhanced with instant messaging technology or executing trades through trusted counterparties. DMA has been adopted by buy-side traders to aggregate liquidity that is fragmented across U.S. execution venues. DMA tools permit buy-side traders to execute multiple venues directly without intervention from brokers. However, the real motivation for DMA trading is cheaper commissions. DMA commissions are about one cent a share, while program trades cost roughly two cents and block trades cost four to five cents per share.

E

Electronic Communication Networks (ECNs)   One of the major advances in providing better access to markets, giving buy-side traders more autonomy, has been Electronic Communication Networks or ECNs. ECNs offer electronic real-time price discovery, which enables buyers and sellers to transact relatively inexpensively with a minimum of intermediation. The Securities and Exchange Commission (SEC) defines the biggest electronic trading systems or Electronic Communication Networks (ECNs) as "electronic trading systems that automatically match buy and sell orders at specified prices."[2] The SEC describes ECNs as integral to modern securities markets. Several ECNs are currently registered in the NASDAQ system, which includes Archipelago, BRASS, Instinet, and Island. ECNs' automated communication and matching systems have led to lower trading costs.

Euronext N.V.   the first genuinely cross-border exchange organization in Europe. It provides services for regulated stock and derivatives markets in Belgium, France, the Netherlands and Portugal, as well as in the U.K. (derivatives only). It is Europe's leading stock exchange based on trading volumes on the central order book. Euronext is integrating its markets across Europe to provide users with a single market that is very broad, highly liquid, and extremely cost effective.

explicit costs   unavoidable costs such as commissions, fees, and taxes, which can significantly alter a fund or stock's portfolio. Taxes are important because some investment strategies expose investors to a much greater tax liability than other strategies. A fund with a long-term-horizon philosophy may have lower transaction costs as well as lower tax implications. Funds that trade frequently may be affected by higher taxes. An accurate measure of an investment strategy is observing after-tax returns and not pre-tax returns.

---

[2] U.S. Securities and Exchange Commission, "Electronic Communication Networks," http://www.sec.gov/answers/ecn.htm.

F

Financial Information Exchange (FIX) Protocol   a series of messaging specifications for electronic communication protocol developed for international real-time exchange of securities transactions in the finance markets. It has been developed through the collaboration of banks, broker-dealers, exchanges, industry utilities institutional investors, and information technology providers from around the world. A company called FIX Protocol, Ltd. was established for this purpose and maintains and owns the specification, while keeping it in the public domain.

H

high-touch trading   trades in which prices are quoted over the phone.

I

implementation shortfall   André Perold defines implementation shortfall as the difference in return between a theoretical portfolio and the implemented portfolio.[3] In a paper portfolio, a portfolio manager looks at prevailing prices, in relation to execution prices in an actual portfolio. Implementation shortfall measures the price distance between the final, realized trade price, and a pre-trade decision price.

implicit cost   the price at which an investor or money manager can purchase an asset (the dealer's asking price) and the price at which you can sell the same asset at the same point in time (the dealer's bid price). The price impact this usually creates by trading an asset pushes up the price when buying an asset and pushes it down while selling.

indicative prices   trades in which prices are published but require manual confirmation,

interdealer systems   allow dealers to execute transactions electronically with other dealers through the fully anonymous services of interdealer brokers.

M

Market Data Rules   designed to promote the wide availability of market data and to allocate revenues to SROs that produce the most useful data for investors. They strengthen the existing market data system, which provides investors in the U.S. equity markets with real-time access to the best quotations and most recent trades in the thousands of NMS stocks throughout

---

[3] André F. Perold, "The Implementation Shortfall: Paper vs. Reality," *Journal of Portfolio Management* 14, no. 3 (Spring 1988).

the trading day. Investors of all types have access to reliable source of information for the best prices in NMS stocks.

Markets in Financial Instruments Directive (MiFID)   MiFID came into effect in April 2004 and will apply to European investment firms and regulated markets by late 2007. The goal of MiFID is to increase transparency and accessibility of markets to ensure price formation and protect investors. It achieves this goal similar to Reg NMS through regulating market transparency, order routing requirements, and best execution. The MiFID will introduce a single market and regulatory regime and be applicable to 25 member states of the European Union.

multidealer systems   provide customers with consolidated orders from two or more dealers and provide customers with the ability to execute from among multiple quotes. Often, multidealer systems display to customers the best bid or ask price for a given security among all the prices posted by participating dealers. These systems also generally allow investors to request quotes for a particular security or type of security from one or more dealers. Participating dealers generally act as principals in transitions. A variety of security types are offered through these systems.

N

NASDAQ stock market   the largest electronic screen-based equities securities market in the United States. With approximately 3,250 companies, it lists more companies and, on average, trades more shares per day than any other U.S. market.

NYSE Group, Inc. (NYSE:NYX)   operates two securities exchanges: the New York Stock Exchange (NYSE) and NYSE Arca (formerly known as the Archipelago Exchange, or ArcaEx), and the Pacific Exchange. The NYSE Group is a leading provider of securities listing, trading, and market data products and services. The NYSE is the world's largest and most liquid cash equities exchange. The NYSE provides a reliable, orderly, liquid, and efficient marketplace where investors buy and sell listed companies' stock and other securities. Listed operating companies represent a total global market capitalization of over $22.9 trillion. In the first quarter of 2006, on an average trading day, over 1.7 billion shares valued over $65 billion were traded on the NYSE.

O

operational risk   the risk of information systems or internal controls resulting in unexpected loss. It can be monitored through examining a series of plausible scenarios. It can be assessed through reviews of procedures, data processing systems, and other operating practices.

operations or back office   Once a transaction has been executed by the front office, the trade-processing responsibility rests with various back-office personnel. The back office is responsible for processing all payments and delivery or receipt of securities, commodities, and written contracts. They are responsible for verifying the amounts and direction of payments that are made under a range of netting agreements.

opportunity cost   the standard deviation of the trading cost. This is a function of trade distribution, stock volatility, and correlation among stocks on a trade list over a given time frame. Traders can determine trading costs for a given strategy. One method of minimizing the cost is by implementing a participation algorithm, which consists of a constant percentage of the daily volume.

Options Price Reporting Authority (OPRA)   provides quote and trade data from the six U.S. options exchanges.

Order Management System (OMS)   OMS collects orders and instructions from various portfolio managers, aggregating them into blocks, managing executions, collecting fills, and performing allocations. The OMS is becoming mainstream among large and medium investment advisors and is viewed as a critical piece of technology.

order routing   the domain of direct market access (DMA) technology providers. It figures out what types of orders and where to send orders in order to receive optimal execution to meet the parameters set by a trading strategy. Some of the leading DMA players are trying to differentiate themselves by expanding into other asset classes or trying to build their own OMS.

P

prepackaged algorithms   Most firms now offer prepackaged algorithms (e.g., pairs, long/short, ETF Arbitrage, VWAP, risk arb, etc.) designed to attract those smaller firms that lack algorithm-building capability. The key to prepackaged algorithms is to ensure that they are flexible enough to enable modifications and customization by the clients.

pre-trade TCR   offers historical and predictive data on price behavior or how a trade position might react to different trading strategies. It can help a buy-side trader justify an execution or help assess performance. The information can provide data on a single stock order or program trade details such as volume, volatility, illiquidity, and other risk characteristics. For single stocks, a trader may analyze a number of different parameters such as the share quantity or the duration of the order. Historical data or predictive modeling may derive estimates of the impact of the order, or price movements.

post-trade TCR   data used to research post-trade analysis, including commissions, market data, and the attributes of the order. After the data is collected, the analysis attempts to piece together the transaction costs and determine their origin. The more detailed the information, the more precise the analysis can be. A high-level overview may show how the trade's execution compares to a particular benchmark, or ideal price; a more detailed analysis goes beyond calculating transaction costs and attempts to show when the costs were incurred or why it happened.

prime brokers   known as providers of technological support, access to markets, and synthetic products and introducers to potential investors. They also provide operational functions for settlements, custody, and reporting for buy-side trades. The main reason why prime brokers carry out custody activity is to facilitate margin-lending activities and the associated movement of collateral. Prime brokers earn their revenue through cash lending to support leverage and stock lending to facilitate short selling. It is increasingly common for prime broker clients to structure trades, utilizing synthetic products and other different asset classes. In the stock-lending business, prime brokers act as an intermediary between institutional lenders and other hedge fund borrowers. In financing equity role, prime brokers act in the role of an intermediary.

program trading   defined by the New York Stock Exchange as "equity securities that encompass a wide range of portfolio-trading strategy involving the purchase or sale of a basket of at least 15 stocks valued at $1 million or more."

R
Regulation National Market System ("Reg NMS")   The implementation of Reg NMS is designed to modernize and strengthen the more than 5,000 listed companies within the NMS. At the time this book was written, the projected deadline when Reg NMS–compliant trading systems must be operational was February 7, 2007. The pilots stocks phase will begin May 21, 2007. This represents $14 trillion in market capitalization trading on nine different market centers. The SEC strengthened the NMS to update antiquated rules and promote equal regulation of different types of stocks and markets while displaying greater liquidity. Regulation NMS includes two amendments designed to disseminate market information, and includes new rules designed to modernize and strengthen the regulatory structure of U.S. equity markets.

request for quote (RFQ) a venue where customers or other dealers retain the ability to accept or refuse a trade request.

S

scheduled crossing model orders in a system which are anonymous to participants; unmatched orders can be canceled, retained to await the next match, or routed to another real-time market for matching.

screen-based trading trades in which prices can be executed on a screen.

Securities Industry Automation Corp (SIAC) In the United States, SIAC operates the New York and American Stock Exchange's automation and communications systems to support trading, market data reporting, and surveillance activities. SIAC also supports the NSCC's nation-wide clearance and settlement systems and it is the systems processor for industry-wide National Market System components, such as CTS, CQS, and ITS. SIAC is jointly owned by the NYSE and AMEX.

self-regulatory organization Under the SEC's oversight, self-regulatory organizations (SROs) regulate trading in U.S. equities. The NYSE and NASD and other regional stock exchanges have set out to enforce rules that regulate their own members.

single-dealer systems allow investors to execute transactions directly with a specific dealer of choice, with the dealer acting as principal in each transaction. Dealers offer access through a combination of third-party providers, proprietary networks, and the Internet.[4]

strategy enablers A new category of technology enablers has emerged to assist in the development of analytics. These enablers assist clients as a foundation for analyzing massive amounts of data to develop new algorithms or modify existing ones. These platforms are also configured for developing pre- and post-trade analytics through real-time and historical data.

Sub-Penny Rule prohibits market participants from displaying, ranking, or accepting quotations in NMS stocks that are priced in an increment of less than $0.01, unless the price of the quotation is less than $1.00. If the price of the quotation is less than $1.00, the minimum increment is $0.0001. The sub-penny proposal is a means to promote greater price transparency and consistency in displayed limit orders.

---

[4] The Bond Market Association, "eCommerce in the Fixed-Income Markets: The 2003 Review of Electronic Transaction Systems," http://www.bondmarkets.com/assets/files/ets_report_1103.pdf.

T

Time-Weighted Average Price (TWAP)   TWAP allows traders to "time-slice" a trade over a certain period of time. Unlike VWAP, which typically trades less stock when market volume dips, TWAP will trade the same amount of stock spread out throughout the time period specified in the order. This is an attractive alternative to trading orders, which are not dependent on volume. This scenario can overcome obstacles such as fulfilling orders in illiquid stocks with unpredictable volume.

trade blotter   functions as the central hub, enabling traders to manage orders/lists; apply various benchmarks on the fly; and keep track of current positions, execution data, confirmations, and real-time P&L.

Trade Reporting and Compliance Engine (TRACE)   On January 23, 2001, the Securities and Exchange Commission (SEC) approved the first major transparency initiative in the OTC secondary corporate bond markets. The National Association of Securities Dealers (NASD) launched the first phase of a three-part initiative that all dealers and interdealers report the prices of corporate bond trades to its Trade Reporting and Compliance Engine (TRACE).

Trade-Through Rule or Order Protection Rule   designed to provide protection against a trade-through for all NMS stocks. A trade-through is defined as executing an order at a price that is inferior to the price of a guaranteed or protected quotation, which can often be a limit order displayed by another trading center. An order protection rule is designed to enhance protection of displayed prices, encourage greater use of limit orders, and contribute to increased market liquidity and depth. It is also designed to promote more fair and vigorous competition among orders seeking to supply liquidity.

Transaction Cost Research (TCR)   defined by the TABB Group as the amount of money spent to open a new position or to close an existing position. Transaction cost analysis started with fulfilling regulatory requirements. It can significantly drag performance, especially for portfolio strategies that include high turnover. All transactions have explicit and implicit costs. Explicit costs are disclosed prior to the trade and include commissions, markups, and other fees. Implicit costs represent the costs that are not determined until after the execution of a trade or set of trades is completed.

V

Volume-Weighted Average Price (VWAP)   VWAP remains the primary benchmark for algorithmic trading. Daily VWAP can be calculated through record of daily stock transactions. VWAP is defined as the dollar amount traded for every transaction (price times shares traded) divided by the total shares traded for a given day. The method of judging VWAP is simple. If the price of a buy order is lower than the VWAP, the trade is considered good; if the price is higher, it is considered poor. Performance of traders is evaluated through their ability to execute orders at prices better than the volume-weighted average price over a given trade horizon.

Index

A

Abel-Noser, 106, 63
ABN Amro, 167
Advanced Execution Services (AES), 2, 61, 72, 127
Access Rule, 125, 126, 128, 132, 140
Actual Portfolio, 54
Advent Moxy, 175
Agency Brokers, 5, 34, 62
Aite Group, 36, 39, 42, 100, 115, 116, 117, 148, 155, 159, 161, 164, 166
Al-Khwarizmi, Abdullah Muhammad Musa, 9
Allen, Franklin, 44
Alternative trading systems (ATS), 129
AMEX, 114, 137
Antares, 176
Apama, 167
API, 172
Application Programming Interface (API), 144
Archipelago, 3, 42, 43, 46, 47, 75, 127
Arrival price, 10, 62, 67, 101
Ashton Technology Group, 59
Automation, 18
Automated Trading Desk (ATD), 35
Average Daily Volume (ADV), 31, 61, 62, 67

B

Babson Capital, 146
Back office, 15, 16, 17, 18, 19
Bank of America, 62, 80, 143, 172
Bank of New York, 36, 143
Bank for International Settlements (BIS), 160
Barclays Global Investors, 53
Bear Stearns, 150, 161, 162
Bergan, Peter, 63
Bid-Ask-Midpoint (BAM), 93
Bid-ask spread, 6, 92, 94, 97
Black box trading, 7, 10, 19, 69, 84, 148, 153, 159
Black Monday, 10
Blind Bid, 33
Block Trading, 29, 30, 31, 34, 77, 80
Bloomberg, 19, 75, 116, 142, 164
Bloomberg Portfolio Order Management System, 176, 177
BNY Brokerage, 35, 62, 80
Bond Desk, 117, 121
Bond Market Association, 111
BondVision, 116
Bourne, Kevin, 69
Brokerage Firms, 5
BrokerTec, 123
BTRD, 61
Bulge bracket, 36, 39, 62, 81

Buy-side, 5, 6, 26, 27, 29, 33, 34, 52, 62, 79, 80, 100, 104
Buy-side trader, 7, 8, 77

C

California Institute of Technology, 96
Charles River Trading System, 177
Charles Schwab, 150
Chicago Board of Trade (CBOT), 49, 70, 155
Chicago Mercantile Exchange, 49
Circuit Breakers, 12, 13
Citigroup, 36, 80, 143, 150
Citisoft, 63
Consolidated Tape Association (CTA), 89
Contrarian, 97
Counterparty, 16, 17
Credit Suisse, 2, 34, 35, 61, 72, 74, 150
Crossing networks, 65
Cross-matching, 119
Currenex, 4, 63, 122

D

Daily Program Trading Report (DPTR), 136
Data management, 19
Decalog, 177
Decimalization, 2, 6, 7, 29, 143
Delaware investments, 146
Depository Trust & Clearing Corporation (DTCC), 89
Deutsche Bank, 167, 172
Direct Market Access (DMA), 25, 26, 27, 34, 63, 71 74, 79, 80, 81, 100, 145, 146, 148, 153, 159, 171, 174
Diversification Effect, 11
Dow Jones, 68
Dow Jones Industrial Average, 10, 12
Duration Averaging, 8
Dynamic hedging, 8

E

EBS, 122, 142
EdgeTrade, 35
Electronic Blue Sheets, 136

Electronic Communication Network (ECN), 7, 22, 24, 39, 40, 43, 45, 71, 72, 75, 76, 77, 78, 79, 112, 118, 122, 123, 138, 145, 146, 147, 148, 152, 155, 157, 163
Elkins-McSherry, 106
eSpeed, 69, 117, 119, 123
Euronext N.V., 47
Explicit costs, 98
Eze Castle Traders Console, 178

F

Fidelity Investments, 3, 92, 104, 150, 161
Fimat International Banque, 170
Financial Information Exchange (FIX) Protocol, 2, 3, 13, 71, 79, 86, 113, 144, 146, 164, 166, 168
First In First Out (FIFO), 70
Fixed Income instruments, 4, 38, 69, 112, 115
FlexTrade, 59, 62, 109, 147, 165, 168
FMCNet, 145
Foreign exchange, 19, 38, 122, 123
Front End System Capture (FESC), 138, 139
Front office, 15, 16, 17
Front running, 44
Future Trade, 35

G

Gilman, Sean, 4, 123
Great Depression, 10
Goldberg, Eric, 3
Goldman Sachs, 34, 43, 61, 62, 72, 150, 161
Goldman Sachs Algorithmic Trading (GSAT), 72
Greifeld, Bob, 48
GT Analytics, 106

H

Hedge Funds, 5, 6, 34, 37, 80, 149, 150, 151, 154, 155, 156, 157, 158, 159, 160, 161, 167
Hedge Fund Research Inc. (HFR), 157
Herring, Richard J., 44

High touch, 100
HSBC, 69
Hybrid Market, 41, 43, 127

I

ICAP, 69, 117, 119
Iceberging, 100
Implementation Shortfall, 10, 53, 55, 56,
    61, 67, 68, 91 101
Implicit costs, 103, 109
Indata, 178
Index Arbitrage, 8
Information Leakage, 65
Interactive Brokers (IB), 74
Interbroker-dealer (IDB), 115
Intermarket Trading System (ITS), 40, 129,
    132, 134
ITG, 35, 59, 61, 62, 68, 106, 108, 143
International Swaps and Derivatives
    Association (ISDA), 122
Instinet, 3, 27, 35, 48, 58, 75

J

JP Morgan, 35, 43, 72, 143, 150,
    167, 172
Journal of Financial Economics, 121

K

Killian, Ray, 143
Kx Systems, 35

L

Latent Zero, 178
Lava Trading, 36, 74, 80, 143, 171
Lehman Brothers, 35, 61 72, 104, 172
Lehman Model Execution (LMX), 72
Leinweber, David J., 96
Levy, Steven, 146
Lime Brokerage, 35
Liquidity Effect, 12

Loeb, Thomas, 94
London Stock Exchange, 13
Long View, 179

M

Macgregor, 145
MacGregor XIP 7s, 179
Madoff, 59
Market Data Rules and Plans, 125, 126,
    128, 133, 140
Market on close (MOC), 101
Markets in Financial Instruments Directive
    in Europe (MiFID), 133, 134
Member Firm Drop Copy (MFDC), 138, 139
Merrill Lynch, 35, 43, 61, 62, 72, 150
Merrill Lynch X-ACT, 72
MFN, 145
Miletus Trading, 35
Momentum strategy, 97
Morgan Stanley, 34, 35, 61, 62, 72, 74, 150
Mutual Funds, 5, 6
Multiple Trading Venues, 65
Muni-Center, 116, 117

N

NASDAQ, 2, 3, 6, 7, 8, 25, 26, 39, 42,
    43, 48, 75, 78, 100, 114, 126, 137, 148, 176
National Association of Securities Dealers
    (NASD), 6, 69, 105, 120, 121, 127,
    135, 137
New York Stock Exchange (NYSE), 6, 8,
    12, 26, 29, 30, 39, 40, 41, 42, 46, 47, 100,
    114, 122, 126, 127, 131, 135, 136, 137,
    138, 140, 168
Neovest, Inc., 172
Nomura, 62
NYFIX, 106
NYSE Rule 123, 137, 138, 148

O

Operational Risk, 16
Options Price Reporting Authority (OPRA),
    87, 88

Order Handling Rule, 71
Order Management Systems (OMS), 19, 22, 24, 25, 27, 36, 112, 145, 146, 152, 164, 172, 174–179
Order Protection Rule, 39, 125, 128, 131, 132, 139
Order routing, 19, 25
Order Submission Rules, 53
Over The Counter (OTC), 15, 40, 43, 46, 111, 115, 120, 127, 136, 171, 172

P

Paper Portfolio, 54
Pegging, 101
Perold, Andre, 54, 91
Piper Jaffray, 61, 62
Plexus Group, 36, 94, 106, 143
Portfolio Insurance, 8, 11
Portware, 3, 35, 108, 165, 169
Post-trade, 21, 24, 53, 54, 68, 86, 103, 105, 134
Pre-trade, 21, 24, 53, 54, 63, 64, 67, 86, 91, 103, 107, 108, 109, 134
Prime Broker, 34, 153, 154, 155, 156, 158, 159, 160, 162
Program Trading, 8, 10, 12, 29, 30, 32, 33, 34, 80, 81, 100
Proprietary trading, 62
Putnam Investments, 92
Putnam, Jerry, 46

Q

Quant House, 170
Quantitative Services Group (QSG), 36, 106, 170

R

Rabbit Portfolio, 54
Radianz, 173
Real Time (TCA), 65
Real-time data, 19
Reconciliation, 18
REDIPlus, 72, 74, 143

Regulation National Market System (NMS), 39, 41, 47, 49, 125, 127, 128, 129, 130, 131, 133, 138, 139, 149
Regulatory Reporting, 24
Request For Quote (RFQ), 69, 123, 125
Reuters, 68, 69, 116, 121, 122, 142, 164
Risk Effect, 11
Rule 390, 39, 43, 44, 45, 46, 49

S

Sales trader, 26
Salomon Brothers, 3
Santayana, Manny, 2
S&P 500, 10, 11, 12
Sarbanes-Oxley, 44
Security Exchange Act of 1934, 43
Securities Exchange Commission (SEC), 2, 6, 7, 10, 47, 75, 125, 126, 128, 130, 134, 135, 136, 137
Securities Industry Automation Corp (SIAC), 83, 87, 89
Self Regulatory Organizations (SRO), 126, 131, 133, 135
Sell-side, 4, 20, 77
Settlements, 15, 17, 18, 27, 43, 89, 153, 154
Slippage, 65
Smart order routing, 22, 101
Soft dollars, 21, 51
Sonic Financial Technologies, 36, 80, 143
Specialist, 43
Speer Leads & Kellog (SLK), 143
Straight Through Processing (STP), 19, 27, 116, 162
Strategy enabler, 19, 85
STN, 36
Sungard, 75, 89, 172, 173, 175
SunGard Transaction Network (STN), 145
Sub-penny Rule, 125, 128, 132, 140
Suutari, Kirsti, 68

T

T. Rowe Price, 146
TABB Group, 21, 72, 75, 81, 84, 87, 103, 104, 131, 144, 153, 155, 158, 160, 163

Tabb, Larry, 144, 163
Telekurs Financial, 121
Thain, John, 46
Thomson, 89, 116, 117, 118, 119
Time slicing, 101
Time Weighted Average Price (TWAP), 10, 60, 62, 101, 150
TowerGroup, 161
Trade Reporting and Compliance Engine (TRACE) Reporting, 70, 120, 121
Trade Through Rule, 39, 125, 131, 132
TradeWeb, 69, 116, 117, 118, 119, 121
Transaction Cost Analysis (TCA), 22, 63, 147
Transaction Cost Research (TCR), 103
Transaction Network Services, Inc. (TNS), 173, 174

U

UBS, 61, 172
UNX, 35, 62
U.S. corporate bonds, 116, 118
U.S. treasuries, 4, 69, 112, 116, 118, 123
User Acceptance Testing (UAT), 183

V

Valentine, Denise, 145
Vhayu Technologies, 35, 166
Volume Weighted Average Price (VWAP), 10, 25, 32, 52, 56, 58, 59, 60, 62, 63, 64, 65, 67, 85, 99, 101, 106, 109, 150, 166, 168, 169, 171

W

Wealth Effect, 11
Wharton, 44

X

Xenomorph, 35, 167

Z

Zero Alpha Group, 92
Zero latency, 83